THE RACIAL POLICIES OF AMERICAN INDUSTRY

REPORT NO. 1

THE NEGRO IN THE AUTOMOBILE INDUSTRY

by

HERBERT R. NORTHRUP

Chairman, Department of Industry
Wharton School of Finance and Commerce
University of Pennsylvania

Published by

INDUSTRIAL RESEARCH UNIT, DEPARTMENT OF INDUSTRY
Wharton School of Finance and Commerce
University of Pennsylvania

Produced and Distributed by
University of Pennsylvania Press
Philadelphia, Pennsylvania 19104

FOREWORD

In September 1966, the Ford Foundation announced a major grant to the Industrial Research Unit of the Wharton School to fund a three-year study of the Racial Policies of American Industry. The purpose of the study is to determine why some industries are more hospitable to the employment of Negroes than are others and why some companies within the same industry have vastly different racial employment policies, and to propose appropriate policy.

The studies have proceeded on an industry-by-industry basis, under the direction of the undersigned, with Dr. Richard L. Rowan, Associate Professor of Industry, as Associate Director. In addition, both Dr. Rowan and the undersigned have undertaken specific industry studies. This study of the automobile industry is the first in a series of reports dealing with particular industries. Studies of the aerospace, iron and steel, pulp and paper, petroleum, rubber tire, insurance, department store, and some fifteen other industries are scheduled to be published during the next few years. We expect during this period also to complete major studies combining and comparing the findings of the various industry studies.

Numerous persons in industry and government have made this study possible, for without their help and courtesy, it obviously could not have been accomplished. They desire anonymity, but deserve much more. Very special thanks are due Dr. John R. Coleman, who, as a staff member of the Ford Foundation, made this grant possible. Helpful comments were received from Professors Richard L. Rowan, William Gomberg, F. Ray Marshall, and Alan B. Batchelder, and from Father Theodore V. Purcell. Manuscript and typing assistance were provided by Mrs. Margaret E. Doyle, Mrs. Helen S. White, and Mrs. Marie P. Spence, and administrative and secretarial functions were also cared for by Mrs. Doyle. Mrs. Marjorie C. Denison and Miss Elsa Klemp did the table calculations, proofreading, and index. Errors or shortcomings, of course, are the responsibility of the undersigned.

Philadelphia
January 1968

HERBERT R. NORTHRUP

TABLE OF CONTENTS

LIST OF TABLES

CHAPTER I.

Introduction

The automobile industry provides the classic example of how the Negro has fared in a dynamic, volatile, yet expanding mass production industry. The extent of Negro employment in the industry is closely related to its growth, but many other factors have been involved: government policy, the impact of a powerful union, and the ideas of America's greatest individualistic entrepreneur, the late Henry Ford. Other influences are also at work. Negro employment in this industry, as in others, is a function of the interaction of numerous pressures which shape the resultant racial policies and alter them significantly over time.

This study is concerned with the development, status, and problems involved in racial employment practices in the automobile industry, and particularly in the three principal companies therein: General Motors, Ford, and Chrysler. Plant visits by the author and most of the research were accomplished during the latter part of 1966 and the first half of 1967. Interviews with a variety of persons accompanied these visits, and information was obtained and evaluated by the author to supplement his past experience studying the same subject in this industry. It is believed that the firsthand information and statistics thus obtained represent an accurate portrayal of the situation in the industry.

CHAPTER II.

The Industry Background

In many ways the automobile industry epitomizes the American economy. Geared to turn out millions of quality products at relatively reasonable prices, it has set the tone and pace for mass production not only in America, but in the world, and changed the lives of all of us who depend upon the motor vehicle. The industry consumes 60 percent of all rubber, 22 percent of all steel and sizeable proportions of other materials.[1] In 1963, 25 percent of all retail sales were automotive, and one business in six was dependent on the manufacture, distribution, servicing, and use of motor vehicles. In 1965, there were 11,750,000 multicar households in the United States, and 79 percent of all American families owned at least one automobile. The following year, Americans traveled 932 billion automobile miles and consumed 75 billion gallons of highway motor fuel. In 1965, a record 11 million motor vehicles—cars, trucks, and buses—produced in the United States were sold.

The automobile has thus taken over the transportation of people and goods. In so doing, it has created great new industries. Such mammoth industries as petroleum, flat glass, rubber, cement, and asphalt depend upon automobile production either for direct sales, or to create their markets. The rise or fall of automobile sales and production is both a barometer of, and an influential factor in, the state of business in America. Where we live and work, the character of our cities, suburbs, and country, the methods of purchasing and the financing of goods have all been significantly altered by the advent of automobile transportation. Its influence is pervasive indeed. Its potential, therefore, for impacting on Negro employment problems is obviously considerable.

---

1. Data on production, sales, etc. are based on figures supplied by the Automobile Manufacturers Association and by Ward's Automotive Reports. The Association prepares an annual "Automobile Facts and Figures" book which is very useful.

2

INDUSTRIAL STRUCTURE

Nearly 200 companies have been engaged in automotive production at one time or another, but today, as for many years, the industry is dominated by three great companies—General Motors Corporation, the Ford Motor Car Company, and the Chrysler Corporation. In 1966, these companies were respectively, the largest, second largest, and fifth largest manufacturing enterprises in the United States. General Motors and Chrysler maintain headquarters in Detroit, Ford in the Detroit suburb of Dearborn.

Over the years, there has been a steady decline in the number of companies in the passenger car business, with American Motors today the only significant domestic competition to the Big Three. Moreover, American has been in a precarious position, holding only 2.5 percent of the market and losing money since 1965. Somewhat greater competition exists in the motor truck and bus portion of the automotive industry. International Harvester, the farm equipment and road machinery manufacturer, is a strong factor in the truck business, as are two independents, White Motor of Cleveland, and Mack Trucks of Allentown, Pennsylvania. In addition, a number of companies manufacture automobile parts and thus compete with captive parts plants of the Big Three.

Nevertheless, the tremendous investments required in tooling, plant, equipment, manpower, and marketing, give the Big Three both awesome competitive advantages and probably preclude any full scale entry into the market. Such investments can probably be recouped only by capturing a greater share of the market than American Motors now holds. Table 1, which gives the basic industrial statistics for the Big Three, and for American Motors, emphasizes this fact. American Motors, which ranked No. 92 among American manufacturing companies in 1966, is not only dwarfed by the size of the Big Three, but lost $12,648,000 despite sales of $870,449,000, assets of $459,502,000, and 27,845 employees!

The automobile industry has retained its huge appetite for manpower despite its tremendous capital investment and despite the great strides in mechanization and automation which have occurred in recent years. In 1966, the United States Bureau of Labor Statistics reported that an average of 859,200 persons were employed in Standard Industrial Classification No. 371—"Motor Vehicles and

TABLE 1.   *The Major Automobile Companies*

Sales, Assets, Net Income, and Employees, 1966

Company	Sales ($000)	Assets ($000)	Net Income ($000)	Employees[a]
General Motors Corp.	20,208,505	12,916,320	1,793,392	745,425
Ford Motor Company	12,240,048	8,090,360	621,023	388,016
Chrysler Corp.	5,649,505	3,148,543	189,223	183,121
American Motors Corp.	870,449	459,502	(12,648)[b]	27,845

Source: *The Fortune Directory,* January 15, 1967
[a] Includes foreign based employees
[b] Loss

Equipment."[2]   Actually the industrial classifications of the federal government are neither uniform as between agencies nor complete in terms of the basic parts plants of the companies. The Bureau of Labor Statistics does not include within SIC 371 automobile stamping, forge, tool and die, foundry castings, or trim shops; the Bureau of the Census includes stamping and trim, but excludes the others.[3]

Consequently, company reports or automobile association statistics provide a better picture of the number of employees who are affected by the racial policies of the companies involved. The data in Table 1, which demonstrate the tremendous size of the Big Three, include foreign based employees, and employees in electrical appliance, aerospace, and other nonautomotive operations of the four companies. The four automobile companies had approximately one million employees in the United States in 1966, the bulk of whom were engaged either in building motor vehicles or parts and equipment for such vehicles.[4]   The size and visibility of this huge labor force obviously give its racial policies great significance.

OCCUPATIONAL DISTRIBUTION

The occupational distribution of employees in the automobile industry is significant for our study. Table 2 shows that distribution for domestic plants of the Big Three in 1966. More than one-half

---

2. As published in the *Monthly Labor Review,* Table A-9.
3. I am indebted to Dr. Donald Irwin, formerly of Chrysler Corporation, for this summary of the deficiencies of SIC 371 for our purposes.
4. The companies are product integrated to various degrees. General Motors, for example, probably manufactures more of its own components than its competitors, but only Ford has its own steelmaking and glassmaking facilities, although Chrysler now has a glass plant.

Table 2. *Total Employment by Occupation Group*

Domestic Plants, Big Three Automobile Companies, 1966

Occupation Group	Number of Employees	Percent of Employees in Each Group
Officials and Managers	74,395	7.9
Professionals	51,053	5.4
Technicians	24,499	2.6
Sales, Office, and Clerical	93,365	9.9
Craftsmen	129,123	13.6
Operatives	515,843	54.4
Laborers	32,352	3.4
Service Workers	26,755	2.8
Total	947,385	100.0

Source: Data in author's possession

These data include most of the nonautomobile manufacturing of the Big Three. The differences in totals with those for 1966 found in Table 9 are probably attributable to differences in payroll week used. Only a few hundred persons classified as "sales" are included in the "sales, office, and clerical" group.

of the employees are classified as "operatives," a basically semiskilled group. Operatives include persons who perform very rudimentary jobs on assembly lines that require only the most meager of on the job instruction, others who perform assembly or machine attendant jobs that require a few weeks instruction before reasonable proficiency is obtained, and still others who work on jobs requiring several months instruction before the required performance and productivity may be expected. Basically, however, these jobs can be readily picked up and require less than a high school education for proficiency.

The next largest group—13.6 percent of the total—are the skilled tradesmen. They include a wide range of crafts requiring considerable training and skill. They are a blue collar elite, highly sought after by the companies. Skills range from the top flight diemaker, to the millwright and welder, and include the whole gamut of metal and woodworking crafts.

Office and clerical staffs are almost 10 percent of the total, and the professional and managerial group continue to increase. Automobile companies employ few sales personnel directly, since selling is done by franchised dealers.[5]

---

5. *Automobile Facts and Figures, 1967*, reported that there were 33,349 franchised passenger car dealers in 1963, including those selling all domestic and foreign manufactured cars.

The blue collar jobs thus continue to predominate in the occupational distribution in the automobile industry, in contrast to such industries as aerospace where salaried employment has equaled or outstripped the hourly work force. Moreover, the bulk of the jobs in the automobile plants lie within a narrow skill range. Essentially unskilled and untried workers can be taken off the streets, with minimal educational, communication, and arithmetic backgrounds, and can be successfully utilized as assembly line workers or taught to be machine tenders in a short period. Of course such persons have limitations on the number and type of jobs that they can fill. Employees with better education, experience, and training have a decided advantage in being more trainable and able to adapt to change. Yet the fact remains that the automobile industry has a capacity far beyond that of many industries to utilize the poorly educated and inexperienced recruit. This, of course, has great significance for Negro workers who are disproportionately represented in the poorly educated strata of society, and who so often have had little prior plant work experience or even exposure to such experience.

WAGES AND EARNINGS

Although the automobile industry can utilize personnel with relatively poor educational and experience backgrounds, the jobs pay well. In 1966 hourly earnings for automotive production workers averaged $3.44 per hour, and weekly earnings, $147.23.[6] General Motors estimated that its production employees enjoyed 30 percent higher straight-time hourly earnings than was the average for production and related workers in all manufacturing establishments in the United States.[7] In 1966, average weekly earnings of production workers in all manufacturing were $112.34, for production workers in durable goods manufacturing, the weekly earnings averaged $122.09. The average hourly earnings for all manufacturing production employees in 1966 were $2.72, for those in durable goods industries, $2.90.[8] General Motors also reported that fringe benefits provided its employees averaged $1.30 per hour during the first

---

6. Data from U. S. Bureau of Labor Statistics, *Monthly Labor Review*, Table C-1.
7. *How Do GM Wages Stack Up?* Pamphlet issued by General Motors Corporation in July 1967.
8. See note 6, *supra.*

quarter of 1967.[9] In 1965, the top five cities in terms of average weekly earnings of production workers were Flint, Detroit, Lansing, Saginaw, and Ann Arbor—all in Michigan and in all of which automotive plants were the major employers.[10]

Since these data were developed, new labor contracts have been negotiated in the industry, providing for substantial increases in wages and benefits for the three years 1968-1971. Automobile workers' wages and benefits will no doubt continue to rank high among those in manufacturing.

UNIONIZATION

These high earnings reflect not only the success and productivity of the industry but also the strength of the union. Organized as the United Automobile Workers in the early 1930's, and now known as the United Automobile, Aerospace and Agricultural Implement Workers, the UAW had a membership of approximately 1,600,000 in 1967. All domestic manufacturing plants of the automobile producers were unionized by the UAW except those in other industries, for example, electrical appliances, which were organized by other unions. Despite energetic efforts by the UAW, the salaried employees of Ford and General Motors remain overwhelmingly nonunion, but many of Chrysler's are found in the UAW fold. The role of the UAW and its leadership in affecting the racial policies of the industry is discussed in later sections of this study.

---

9. See note 7, *supra.*
10. U. S. Bureau of Labor Statistics, Bulletin No. 1370-3, June 1966.

CHAPTER III.

The Pre-World War II Period

In 1910, the U. S. Bureau of the Census reported that the fledgling "motor vehicle" and "motor vehicle bodies and parts" industries employed 105,758 persons, but only 569 Negroes. Twenty years later, total employment stood at 640,474, and Negro employment at 25,895, or 4 percent in 1930 as compared with 0.5 percent twenty years earlier.

The increase in the number and percentage of Negro automobile workers was the result of the shortage of labor which developed during and after World War I. With immigration cut off, first by the War, and later by restrictive legislation, automobile manufacturers, like those in many other industries, commenced extensive recruiting in the South. Thousands of Negroes, and many more southern whites, migrated North to find permanent jobs in automobile, steel, meat packing, and other industries. In many industries, Negro recruits were used as strike breakers. Unionization, however, despite a very brief flurry during World War I which did not affect the major producers, was not a serious threat to the automobile companies, prior to 1934.[11] Negroes were not, therefore, introduced into the industry under strike conditions.

EARLY AREA AND JOB CONCENTRATIONS

This early period also saw the beginning of a trend still extant—much heavier utilization of Negro labor in the Detroit area especially, but also in other urban Michigan plants, than in most plants in other states.[12] Thus, the 1930 census found Negroes comprised 8.7 percent

---

11. On this point, see Sidney Fine, *The Automobile Under the Blue Eagle* (Ann Arbor, Michigan: University of Michigan Press, 1963), pp. 21-30.

12. The story of this early period is based largely upon an unpublished manuscript in the author's possession which Dr. Lloyd H. Bailer prepared for the "Negro in America" study which was directed by Dr. Gunnar Myrdal; and on the author's field work in the Detroit area during World War II.

of Michigan's automobile labor force, 2.4 percent of Indiana's, 1.9 percent of Ohio's, and few elsewhere. The reasons for this early Michigan concentration appear to be (1) the location in that state of the type of work for which Negroes were utilized; (2) the fact that no labor shortage existed where plants in other states were built and staffed; and (3) the policies of Henry Ford, the bulk of whose operations were in the Detroit area.

In 1940, Dr. Lloyd H. Bailer, after a detailed study of Negroes in the automobile industry, reported that:

> . . . the vast majority of Negro automobile workers are employed in the foundry, paint, and maintenance departments (chiefly as janitors) or as general unskilled labor. Of these, . . . the foundry is the most important. In fact, one can be quite certain that an automobile plant employing a sizable portion of Negro labor has a foundry. In many large plants the foundry is known as a "black department." In general, foundry occupations are the most undesirable in the industry . . . hot, dirty, and demand exceptional strength. The accident rate is higher in the foundry than any other department. . . . These conditions are not restricted to foundries in the automobile industry but are characteristic of all foundries . . . automobile foundries are among the safest and most modern. . . . But . . . foundry work is extremely disagreeable and often dangerous.[13]

In addition to foundry work, Negroes were heavily concentrated as sanders and sprayers in paint departments. Again these were (and are) undesirable jobs, arduous and unpleasant. And, of course, Negroes were widely used as janitors, porters, laborers, cafeteria bus boys, etc.

Because most foundry and body plants of automobile companies were (and are) located in Michigan, this tended to increase the proportion of Negroes in this state's industry. Some companies, according to Bailer, used Negroes in Michigan foundries and body shop paint departments, but not in these jobs in other states. Even in Michigan, however, foundries and paint departments were not all Negro. A lot of Mexican and other foreign born whites were also employed in these jobs, which were often 30 to 50 percent Negro. Some jobs, for example, chippers and foundry laborers, were often very nearly all Negro.

Dr. Bailer also found, in plants other than those of Ford, which are treated separately below, six Negro foremen and a "few" Negro

---

13. *Ibid.,* pp. 43-45.

straw bosses. These Negro foremen supervised all Negro groups. In most cases, however, supervisors were white even when the force in the department was over one-half Negro.

GENERAL MOTORS AND CHRYSLER

Dr. Bailer found that Negroes were not used on the assembly lines prior to World War II even in Michigan, except at Ford as will be discussed below. The general occupational and plant employment patterns reserved the assembly line for whites and confined Negroes in assembly plants to janitors, cafeteria workers, or laborers off the line. The reasons seem to be the general feeling of the times that whites would not work with Negroes, unless the work was so unpleasant or degrading that only a very poor class of whites was involved, as in foundries; or that Negroes were incapable or unsuited to such work. In this regard, of course, the automobile industry was typical of industry in general of the period.

According to Mr. Louis G. Seaton, Vice-President, General Motors Corporation, Dr. Bailer's findings omitted some significant developments at General Motors:

> Negro employees were placed on inspection, machining and assembly operations in General Motors as early as 1933. Cadillac, Chevrolet, and Oldsmobile were leaders in this effort in Michigan. In 1936, for instance, 30% of the employees working on inspection and machining operations at the Chevrolet Gear & Axle Plant in Detroit were Negroes.
>
> Both Cadillac and Oldsmobile had Negro employees in skilled trades classifications prior to World War II and 4% of the Oldsmobile work force in Lansing was composed of Negroes who were employed on production jobs in the early 30's. A number of these Negroes were on higher rated jobs such a paint spray, dingman, sheet metal finisher, polisher, auto mechanic, auto repairman and final inspector. . . .[14]

It does appear that despite the interesting developments in the divisions noted by Mr. Seaton, Negroes at General Motors were heavily concentrated in the foundry departments. Thus Bailer estimated that about 2,500 of General Motors' 100,000 employees in Michigan and Indiana were Negroes, and that about 2,000 of these worked in foundries in Flint, Saginaw, and Pontiac. But General Motors obviously did not follow so strict a policy of confining Negroes to the

---

14. Letter to author from Mr. Louis G. Seaton, August 31, 1967.

traditional jobs which the industry reserved for them, as Bailer indicated, and permitted some mixing of the races on machines, and in departments.

Actually Negro employment policies at General Motors prior to World War II were apparently left at least largely to decentralized management decisions. As Mr. Seaton noted, Oldsmobile, Chevrolet, and Cadillac were willing to pioneer in several plants. On the other hand, the Fisher Body Division went to the other extreme. Its management apparently did not believe in employing Negroes, for its plants prior to World War II often did not have even a Negro janitor. The reasons for this wide divergency of practice during the 1930's, other than managerial policy of the various General Motors divisions and plants, are not apparent.

During the 1920's, the automobile industry established a number of assembly plants on the East Coast, in the South and Southwest, and on the Pacific Coast. These plants employed virtually no Negroes. In some areas, Negro labor was not available. In other areas, there was no labor shortage when plants were constructed, so that no practice of employing Negro labor was established. The plants built in the South and Southwest followed the practice initiated by the textile industry in the latter part of the nineteenth century: all basic factory jobs, mechanical or assembly, were manned by whites. A few Negroes were hired as janitors, outside laborers, or cafeteria bus boys, but basically the prewar automobile plants in the South employed whites only. General Motors, Chrysler, and Ford all followed the policy outside of Michigan and its contiguous areas of avoiding racial problems by not hiring Negroes except in the few service or laboring occupations. This policy was facilitated by the fact that nearly all foundries were located in Michigan or neighboring states.

The Chrysler Corporation had far fewer parts plants of its own prior to World War II than either of its major competitors. Dr. Bailer estimated that only 2,000 of its 50,000 employees in 1940 were Negroes, nearly all of whom were found in Michigan plants. Chrysler's Negro employees were then almost all confined to the traditional jobs reserved for them in the industry: the foundry, especially at the Main Dodge plant, and in painting and laboring jobs.[15]

Prior to World War II, Chrysler bought its bodies from the Briggs Manufacturing Corporation (which it acquired after World War II).

---

15. These data are all based on figures given to Dr. Bailer by company and plant managements.

TABLE 3. *Negro Workers in Major Automobile Companies*
First Quarter, 1940

Company	Total Hourly Workers	Negro Workers	Percent Negro
Ford Motor Company[a]	88,773	9,882	11.1
Briggs Mfg. Corporation[a]	14,000	3,000	21.4
General Motors Corporation[b]	100,000	2,500	2.5
Chrysler Corporation	50,000	2,000	4.0
Packard Motor Car Company	16,000	600	3.8

Source: Lloyd H. Bailer, 1940 unpublished MS, based on data given him by companies.
[a]Michigan plants only.
[b]Michigan and Indiana automobile and auto parts plants only.
Note: Briggs has since been acquired by Chrysler.

Briggs had the highest percentage of Negro employees in the industry —3,000 out of a total of 14,000, or 21.4 percent. (See Table 3.) All the Negro employees of Briggs were found in Michigan; it had no Negro employees in its Indiana plant.

MR. FORD WAS UNIQUE

As was the case in so many aspects of his business life, Henry Ford's policies toward Negro labor were unique. At the mammoth River Rouge plant in Dearborn, a Detroit suburb, Ford employed the largest number of Negro workers in the industry. Indeed, about 40 percent of all Negro automobile workers worked at River Rouge. And although there were similar overconcentrations of Negroes in the foundry, the paint department, and in unskilled jobs at River Rouge as existed elsewhere in the industry, Negroes were employed during this period in nearly all manufacturing departments as well.

Ford's Negro employment policies grew out of representations made to him by members of the Negro community, particularly Negro ministers, after World War I. During the 1921 depression, the Negro leaders saw workers of their race losing newly gained industrial jobs, and appealed to Mr. Ford to give consideration to the needs of Detroit's new Negro population. He responded by agreeing to keep the percentage of Negro factory workers in his main facility—then Highland Park, but soon thereafter River Rouge—roughly proportionate to the Negro population ratio in Detroit. When the great River Rouge works was opened in the twenties, Negroes moved with their jobs and more were hired.

TABLE 4. *Negro Workers in Ford Michigan Plants*
1939-1940

Plant	Total Hourly Workers	Negro Workers	Percent Negro
River Rouge	84,096	9,825	11.7
Lincoln	2,332	31	1.3
Highland Park	992	16	1.6
Ypsilanti	805	9	1.1
Flat Rock	548	1	0.2

Source: Lloyd H. Bailer, 1940 unpublished MS, based on data given him by Ford payroll department.
Note: Ford then had 14 other small Michigan plants, none of which employed Negroes.

Table 3 shows the automobile companies employing the largest number of Negroes in the 1934-1940 period. Over half were accounted for by Ford, although Briggs had the highest percentage. Table 4 shows the distribution as among Ford plants. River Rouge employed nearly all the Negroes in the company. Most Negroes once employed at Highland Park were moved to River Rouge; Ford did not change the policies of the Lincoln Company when he purchased it in the early 1920's; and Negroes were not recruited for assembly plants in Norfolk, Memphis, Atlanta, Dallas, St. Louis, the East Coast,

TABLE 5. *Distribution of Negro Employees,*
Ford River Rouge Works
October 1937

Division	Total Hourly Workers	Negro	Percent Negro
Foundry	12,254	4,659	38.0
Foundry Machine Shop	3,952	616	15.6
Motor Mfg. & Assembly	14,577	754	5.2
Chassis & Parts Mfg. & Assembly	9,468	564	6.0
Spring & Upset Machining	5,484	574	10.5
Steel Stamping	7,046	555	7.9
Rolling Mills & Blast Furnaces	8,193	1,182	14.4
Tool Rooms	5,131	51	1.0
Construction	3,515	232	6.6
Miscellaneous	14,476	638	4.4

Source: Lloyd H. Bailer, 1940 unpublished MS, from data given him by Ford payroll department.

or Northern Michigan. At River Rouge, however, Ford kept his bargain with the Negro community and kept it well.

Table 5 shows the distribution of Negroes working at River Rouge as of October 5, 1937. As already noted, Negroes were unduly concentrated in unskilled and foundry jobs, and received a smaller than proportionate share of some of the better jobs. But the significant fact is that the River Rouge plant was the key one in the industry where Negroes were given the opportunity to work on nearly all operations pertinent to the industry. At River Rouge Negroes worked on the assembly line in large numbers; there alone were Negro apprentices and trade school graduates accepted; River Rouge had the industry's only Negro tool and die mechanics; and it had the industry's largest and most significant aggregation of parts assemblers, and of machine and press operators. Moreover, River Rouge had more Negro supervisors than were found in the rest of the industry, and the only ones supervising racially mixed crews.

The significance of the River Rouge operation on Negro employment transcended the automobile industry. When Henry Ford built this huge complex, he determined to make his operations as self-sufficient as possible. The River Rouge operations include not only an engine plant, stamping and other parts plants, and an assembly plant, but also huge blast furnaces and rolling mills where Ford makes its own steel; later a glass plant (Ford is the third largest flat glass maker in the country); foundries, docks where Ford-owned Great Lakes carriers unload coal, iron ore, and other raw materials; and at one time a cement plant, a tire plant, a lumber mill, and a paper box factory. Negroes were employed in all these plants, although in some areas, such as the rolling mill and the glass plant, they were not working on key jobs. In addition, at Ford, Negroes and whites commonly worked together in mixed pairs on presses and on other machines, as well as on assembly and subassembly lines. In short, prior to World War II, Negroes came closer to job equality at the Ford River Rouge works than they did at any large enterprise known to the author or recorded in the literature.

Ford fostered racial job equality with his typical combination of authoritarianism and paternalism. If white workers did not like his racial employment policies, their only alternative was to leave. Having made up his mind that his policies were proper, he brooked no interference nor gave any heed to the racial antagonisms on account of which most other employers feared to mix races or to give Negroes opportunities for better jobs.

In order to see that his policies were carried out, two Negroes were attached to the Ford Service Department, a combination of plant personnel and security force. They were responsible for recruiting and employing Negroes, and Negroes who felt that they had been discriminated against or otherwise aggrieved or who had problems, could take their cases directly to their Service Department representatives. That the Negro representatives in the Service Department had authority to correct situations was demonstrated sufficiently well so that line supervisors tended to carry out the Ford policy.

The fact that Ford offered Negroes the best jobs in the Detroit area gave Ford not only the choice Negro applicants, but also tremendous community leverage. This became a matter of consequence with the use of unionism which Henry Ford fought with his typical determination.

THE INITIAL UNION IMPACT

After the election of Franklin D. Roosevelt and the passage of the National Industrial Recovery Act (NRA) in 1933, automobile workers attempted to form unions, but with limited success in the face of employer opposition, the insistence of the American Federation of Labor on organization along craft lines, the inexperience of the budding unionists, and the inability of NRA boards to enforce their orders. According to a careful history of the NRA period:

> . . . The presence of a considerable number of Negroes and foreign-born in the automobile plants, particularly in the Detroit area, also posed a problem for the A. F. of L. The opposition of the Negro to the Federation because of the racial discrimination practiced by some of its affiliates, the racial antagonism between Negro and white workers in the automobile plants, the Negro support for the antiunion Ford Motor Company, which employed more Negroes than any other automobile firm and discriminated against them less in the assignment of jobs, and the higher rate of unemployment among Negroes than among white automobile workers all deterred the Negroes from responding to union entreaties.[16]

The same historian reports that American Federation of Labor's chief Detroit organizer noted that Negroes "were not coming to his meetings and that it was a 'tremendous problem' to persuade them to join the [AFL] federal labor unions."[17]

---

16. Fine, *op. cit.*, p. 149.
17. *Ibid.*

When unionism did come to the automobile industry in the mid-1930's, Mr. Ford was again unique. He held out against acceptance after General Motors, Chrysler, and most independents had recognized the United Automobile Workers, then an affiliate of the new Committee for Industrial Organization, in the wake of sit-down strikes and government intervention. Unionism under the UAW banner officially accepted Negroes as members without discrimination, but did nothing immediately to alter racial employment trends. The UAW leadership, traditionally split before Walter Reuther achieved control in the late 1940's, was in no position to alter the employment *status quo*. Seniority agreements were largely based on departmental and occupational groupings, and hence did little to promote greater integration. In some southern and border state plants, the national union officials had all that they could do even to gain union membership for Negro laborers and janitors in the face of the opposition of white members and local union leadership.[18]

The campaign to unionize Ford put the spotlight on the race issue. As one of its responses to the union campaign, Ford stepped up its employment of Negroes, and made much of the fact that Negroes were in a superior position at River Rouge than elsewhere. When the UAW struck River Rouge in 1941, some violence occurred between Negroes loyal to Ford and white strikers. Later Negroes heavily supported Ford's attempted deal with a rival American Federation of Labor group, but the UAW won handily in an election conducted by the National Labor Relations Board.

Ford turned from bitter antiunionism to complete union acceptance with a compulsory union shop. For the first time, the bulk of Negro automobile workers became union members, and a significant force in the UAW. Yet as the war drew close, Negroes were far from integrated into the union. In a careful study, published in 1944, Dr. Bailer found that Negro participation in union affairs was considerably less than whites because of a variety of causes, the three most significant of which were their traditionally unhappy experience with the older craft unions, the seniority system, and the lack of social acceptance.[19]

The first point—traditional union opposition to Negro membership—is exemplified by the building and railroad union practices

---

18. A discussion of UAW policies toward Negroes in the immediate pre-World War II and early war period is found in Herbert R. Northrup, *Organized Labor and the Negro* (New York: Harper and Brothers, 1944), Chapter IX.
19. Lloyd H. Bailer, "The Automobile Unions and Negro Labor," *Political Science Quarterly*, Vol. LIX (December 1944), pp. 548-577; and especially pp. 556-562.

which are still antagonistic to Negro advancement.[20] UAW locals, of course, put no bars on Negro membership—except in the South. White members of the Atlanta, Georgia, local attempted to have all Negroes—then used only as laborers and janitors—discharged. The UAW national leadership found itself helpless to force the local to admit the Negroes, but stood firm against any demand for their discharge.[21]

The seniority system deserves further comment. Since Negroes were concentrated in the lower rated jobs, they could be displaced by white workers with better jobs and higher seniority when the labor force contracted, as it did in 1938. But when expansion occurred, Negroes desiring upgrading found that union contracts were often ignored because to do otherwise would result in the admission of Negroes to existing all white occupations or departments or to jobs traditionally reserved for whites. Convention debates and other sources cited by Bailer or found by the present author leave no doubt that, although the national officers of the UAW were generally sympathetic to Negro advancement, local officials who needed white worker support for re-election, generally helped to maintain the *status quo*, and the national officers did not feel that they could intervene. It is, therefore, not surprising that Dr. Bailer found that the Negro automobile worker trusted Henry Ford more than the leaders of the UAW, or that Negroes on a number of occasions went through UAW picket lines during strikes at various companies.[22]

The economic situation was acerbated by social affronts. Local meetings and some national conventions were held where Negroes were denied service. Local union social affairs were held with Negroes snubbed, or affairs were cancelled if Negroes showed a disposition to attend.[23] Despite the firmest of resolutions annually enacted by the national UAW convention, and despite a firm commitment to nondiscrimination by R. J. Thomas, then president of the UAW, and if anything, a firmer belief in equality by his successor, and then a UAW vice-president, Walter Reuther, it was apparent that the racial employment pattern and race relations in the industry were at an uneasy *status quo* at the time that America was thrust into World War II.

---

20. See Northrup, *op. cit.*, Chapters II and III; and F. Ray Marshall, *The Negro and Organized Labor* (New York: John Wiley & Sons, Inc., 1965), *passim*.
21. Interview of this author with ex-UAW Atlanta local president, June 12, 1940.
22. Bailer, "Automobile Unions and Negro Labor," *op. cit.*, pp. 562-566 for discussion of seniority system, and pp. 550-556 for details of unrest.
23. *Ibid.*, pp. 560-562.

CHAPTER IV

The World War II Period

The shift over of the automobile industry from passenger cars to aircraft, tanks, army trucks, and other ordnance threatened initially to be disadvantageous to Negro workers. Worker shortages occurred first in skilled and assembly jobs from which Negroes had been barred in most facilities and fear was expressed that foundry and paint work would be in less demand. Most managements were disinclined to train Negroes for new jobs. Past experience had taught them that white workers would not work with Negroes on assembly lines or machine jobs, and they felt that only trouble would result from attempts to mix the races. White dominated local union leadership often reinforced these prejudices.[24]

Ford, too, followed its traditional policies, which were, of course, quite different from those of the rest of the industry. Negro foundry workers were trained and upgraded at River Rouge without governmental prodding, as were other employees in that huge works. On the other hand, Ford also followed its non-River Rouge racial employment policies at the new Willow Run bomber plant. Located in what was then a rural area, and reachable only by car, with little housing then nearby, Willow Run employed few Negroes in any capacity.

WARTIME CHANGES IN MANAGEMENT POLICIES

Both the failure to upgrade Negroes, and more often, actually doing so, caused wartime work stoppages. Negro laborers and foundry workers at Chrysler's Dodge Main Plant struck in August 1941 because they were being passed over in transfers to the Chrysler Tank Arsenal. Governmental pressure forced both the company and the local union to change their attitudes and transfers were initiated.

---

24. This section is based on Northrup, *Organized Labor and the Negro, loc. cit.,* and Bailer, "The Automobile Unions and Negro Labor," *loc. cit.*

Strikes occurred at Packard and Hudson, among other plants, over Negro upgrading. At first such strikes caused management to backtrack. But as the labor market tightened, government pressure increased, the national UAW obtained greater control over its locals and management became more experienced, such outbursts were dealt with more firmly. In mid-1942, for example, a demonstration against Negro employment and upgrading at the Dodge Main Plant resulted in no change of company policy—now committed to an expansion and upgrading of Negroes—and the discharge of the leaders of the agitation.

The worst racial strike occurred at the Packard plant, in the heart of Detroit in June 1943. It had been preceded by minor disturbances over Negro upgrading, and shut down the entire works. Although both national and local union leaders tried to control the situation, many shop stewards were among the strike leaders. Nevertheless, the united stand of unions, company, and government broke the strike in less than one week without concession.

On June 21 of the same year, the worst race riot in Detroit's history to that date commenced. No violence occurred in the plants —a tribute to both the industry and union leaders. Yet "unionists of both races did participate in the frenzy that raged in various parts of the city."[25] Unlike the similar horror 24 years later, this riot featured white males looting and beating in the Negro areas.

Despite the violence and obstacles, great progress occurred in the turbulent World War II days. Briggs, for example, then an independent company, but now part of the Chrysler organization, increased its percentage of Negroes and integrated them into all manufacturing jobs. Heretofore, they had been confined to paint departments or to unskilled work. Moreover, Briggs employed substantial numbers of Negro women, a group even Ford had not utilized. By a careful indoctrination program Briggs avoided major difficulties in achieving this goal.

Negroes made great progress in both Chrysler and General Motors. As they flocked into the motor city, they found the center city concentrated Chrysler plants the most accessible. Chrysler responded by hiring and upgrading on a vast scale so that by the end of the war it was to have the highest proportion of Negroes in the industry.

At General Motors, large scale upgrading and new hiring also oc-

---

25. Bailer, *loc. cit.*, p. 571.

curred. The traditionally more liberal components—Chevrolet, Cadillac, and Oldsmobile—expanded their programs. The first Negro apprentices of the Corporation were employed by Oldsmobile. Negroes emerged from their foundry and labor status at Buick and Pontiac to win other production jobs. The policies of the Fisher Body Division were also liberalized. Following a hearing of the President's Committee on Fair Employment Practice in Chicago in 1944, which found some discriminatory employment practices at General Motors facilities there, the Corporation adopted a much stronger corporate-wide stance on integration rather than leaving the problem totally to decentralized management.

At the River Rouge works, the situation also changed before the end of the war. The numbers and percentage of Negroes rose there too, as the labor market tightened, but Ford officials were clearly disenchanted by the caliber of Negro recruits available from 1943 until the end of the war. Previously, Ford could take its pick of one of every four Negroes who applied, but as barriers elsewhere dropped and the labor market tightened, all employers found only recent arrivals from the South available. For a time Ford ceased to employ Negroes; and its special Negro representatives in the service department were transferred and not replaced. Henceforth, Negroes at River Rouge were dependent on the union or outside civil rights organizations to handle their special problems when they felt management was unfair.

AREA DIFFERENCES

As before World War II, the greatest advances in Negro employment were made in the Detroit area, and in other Michigan communities. Likewise, in Chicago and Cleveland, considerable progress in overcoming barriers resulted from the combination of a tight labor market, Negro and governmental pressure, and general enlightening of management policies. Patterns of employment in the East and West Coast automobile plants changed less, and in the South very little. But the significant thing is that by the postwar conversion period, despite strife, some nasty incidents, and occasional local management or local union footdragging, Negroes were working on assembly lines, on machines, and in many other jobs alongside whites as a general practice rather than something which only Henry Ford dared to do prior to the war.

On the other hand, by the end of the war there was little progress toward integrating Negroes in white collar and professional positions, or as dealers or dealer salesmen. Moreover, the automobile companies did little, if any, pioneering in southern automobile plants in this period. Developments in these areas would have to wait another two decades.

CHAPTER V

From Post-War Reconversion to 1960

Reconversion resulted in some layoffs and loss of employment for Negroes and whites in the automobile industry, but recovery was rapid as new prosperity and pent up consumer demand kept sales and employment in the industry high through the remainder of the 1940's. Employment was further buoyed by the Korean War demands on the industry in the early 1950's, but slackened demand in 1954 and a serious recession in 1958 cut deeply into employment and into Negro work opportunities for the final years of the decade. An examination of the experience of the major companies in employing Negroes highlights the events of these fifteen years.

THE CHRYSLER EXPERIENCE, 1946-1960

Chrysler emerged from World War II with the largest percentage of Negro employees in the industry. Its concentration in the central Detroit area, its acquisition of the Briggs plants also located there, and its successful integration of the work force during the war caused it to pass Ford in percentage of Negro employees, although not in total numbers of Negroes employed. In 1946, 17 percent of Chrysler's 71,000 employees were Negro.[26]

Negroes continued to gain at Chrysler in the prosperous years after World War II, especially in the Detroit area plants, although as was the case in most automobile plants, such gains were confined, with very few exceptions, to production jobs. A few Negroes were employed as skilled tradesmen or apprentices, and a handful in white collar occupations, but generally these jobs remained closed to Negroes during the 1950's.

In the Detroit area, Chrysler employed over 100,000 persons by the end of 1952, of whom 22 percent were Negroes. At this time, 13.5 percent of Detroit's population was nonwhite. The percentage

---

26. From a reply of Chrysler Corporation to an inquiry of the Social Science Department, Fisk University, September 1946.

of Negroes was less in Chrysler plants outside of the motor city; for example, it was 7.5 percent in the Plymouth assembly plant at Evansville, Indiana, in the late 1950's, where the Negro population ratio was 6 percent. Chrysler has no southern automobile plants, but in border areas such as Evansville, Newark, Delaware, or St. Louis, it did not hesitate to use Negroes in all production jobs.[27]

Chrysler had some difficult times in the 1950's. Corporate employment peaked at 176,356 in 1955, and had not risen that high by 1968. It fell 32,000 in 1956, and by the end of 1958 plummeted to 91,678. Negro employees, being relatively new, were hit disproportionately hard. In 1957, for example, employment at four Chrysler Detroit plants stood at 45,584, including 9,242 Negroes, or 20.3 percent Negro. The following year, these plants employed only 22,776 persons, of whom 3,345, or just 14.7 percent were Negro. Improvement in the Negro workers' status was obviously not possible in this situation until prosperity returned—and for Chrysler, it did not return on a lasting basis until 1962.

FORD IN THE FORTIES AND FIFTIES

The period after World War II was one in which the Ford Motor Company sought successfully to regroup and modernize its operations in order to regain the number two slot in the industry, and even to challenge General Motors for first place. Henry Ford's paternalism was replaced by modern managerial rule; the River Rouge complex was reduced drastically in size, and manufacturing operations decentralized; small assembly plants were closed and fewer larger ones built. The impact on Negro labor was mixed.

The reduction in size of the River Rouge works reduced the Negro percentage in the company, for although production operations in such states as Ohio were well integrated, Rouge had in the 1950's, as it does today, the largest number and percentage of Negroes in the Ford Company. On the other hand, the closing of the small assembly plants in Upper Michigan, which had no Negro employees, or the Memphis plant in which Negroes were confined to a few menial jobs, or of small assembly plants in the East, did not materially reduce Negro employment opportunities.

---

27. Data in this and the ensuing section, unless otherwise indicated, are based on a variety of sources including studies made by various governmental agencies for the President's Committee on Government Contracts (Nixon Committee) during the Eisenhower Administration.

TABLE 6. *Employment by Race*

Ford Motor Company, Twelve Assembly Plants, 1957 and 1958

Plant Location and Date	All Employees			Salaried Employees			Hourly Employees		
	Total	Total Negro	Percent Negro	Total	Total Negro	Percent Negro	Total	Total Negro	Percent Negro
Atlanta									
1957	1,588	21	1.3	227	0	0.0	1,361	21	1.5
1958	1,393	20	1.4	221	0	0.0	1,172	20	1.7
Chicago									
1957	2,230	745	33.4	390	70	17.9	1,840	675	36.7
1958	1,770	515	29.1	330	40	12.1	1,440	475	33.0
Dallas									
1957	2,991	9	0.3	491	0	0.0	2,500	9	0.4
1958	1,652	5	0.3	304	0	0.0	1,348	5	0.4
Detroit									
1957	5,300	807	15.2	1,300	7	0.5	4,000	800	20.0
1958	4,050	681	16.8	1,100	6	0.5	2,950	675	22.9
Los Angeles									
1957	1,715	110	6.4	182	3	1.6	1,533	107	7.0
1958	1,207	90	7.5	280	4	1.4	927	86	9.3
Louisville									
1957	3,525	197	5.6	425	1	0.2	3,100	196	6.3
1958	2,573	158	6.1	420	1	0.2	2,153	157	7.3
Mahwah, N. J.									
1957	5,400	1,160	21.5	650	33	5.1	4,750	1,127	23.7
1958	4,375	921	21.1	475	19	4.0	3,900	902	23.1
Memphis									
1957	1,458	35	2.4	219	0	0.0	1,239	35	2.8
1958	929	23	2.5	181	0	0.0	748	23	3.1
Norfolk									
1957	1,626	9	0.5	249	0	0.0	1,377	9	0.6
1958	1,487	9	0.6	238	0	0.0	1,249	9	0.7
Chester, Pa.									
1957	1,990	141	7.1	281	0	0.0	1,709	141	8.3
1958	1,460	160	11.0	231	0	0.0	1,229	160	13.0
10 Total									
1957	27,823	3,234	11.6	4,414	114	2.6	23,409	3,120	13.3
1958	20,896	2,582	12.4	3,780	70	1.9	17,116	2,512	14.7
Kansas City									
1957	2,250	200	8.9	250	0	0.0	2,000	200	10.0
Metuchen									
1957	1,838	135	7.3	328	0	0.0	1,500	135	9.0
12 Total									
1957	31,911	3,569	11.2	4,992	114	2.3	26,909	3,455	12.8

Source: Reports to the President's Committee on Government Contracts (Nixon Committee).

Note: There are obviously some small arithmetical errors in these data since they do not add up in both directions. These errors do not change the overall results.

Negroes gained some at Ford during the post-World War II period partially because Ford expanded sales and employment fairly steadily until 1957, when a pre-1964 peak of 191,759 employees was reported. But even with the 1958 recession, which caused a cutback of 50,000 employees, Negroes were not hurt disproportionately in many cases as Table 6 demonstrates.

In the ten assembly plants surveyed in both 1957 and 1958, the ratio of Negro employment to total employment shows a slight increase despite 7,000 layoffs. More likely, the ratio stayed about constant, for the reported increase in the number of Negroes in the Chester, Pennsylvania plant from 141 to 160 while employment in that plant (since abandoned) fell from 1,990 to 1,460, is more likely a reporting error than a fact. Table 6 does indicate, however, the strong seniority position of Negroes at Ford. At many of these plants, Negroes were either hired when they were opened in the post-World War II era, or for older plants, during the war. At River Rouge also, for which Negro employment exceeded 30 percent of the 35,000 employees, layoffs in the 1958 recession seemed to have affected Negroes about proportionately, rather than excessively, because of the Negroes' strong seniority position there.

Table 6 also reveals that Negroes had made gains as salaried workers in two plants—Chicago and Mahwah, New Jersey. Ford continued to have the most Negro supervisors in the industry, but like its principal competitors, had comparatively few other white collar workers.

Finally, data in Table 6 demonstrates that little progress had been made in opening employment opportunities for Negroes in Ford's southern assembly plants in this period.

GENERAL MOTORS, 1946-1960

General Motors employs the largest number of Negroes in the industry, but a smaller percentage than either Chrysler or Ford. It is likely that General Motors' domestic labor force of about 450,000 in the mid-1950's, was approximately 8 or 9 percent Negro.[28]

---

28. For a good statement of General Motors policy by the staff official responsible for it, see Harold S. McFarland, "Minority Group Employment at General Motors," in Herbert R. Northrup and Richard L. Rowan (eds.), *The Negro and Employment Opportunity* (Ann Arbor: Bureau of Industrial Relations, University of Michigan, 1965), pp. 131-136.

TABLE 7. *Employment by Race*

General Motors Corporation, Twelve Assembly Plants, 1957 and 1958

Plant Location and Date	All Employees			Salaried Employees			Hourly Employees		
	Total	Total Negro	Percent Negro	Total	Total Negro	Percent Negro	Total	Total Negro	Percent Negro
Atlanta									
1957	1,676	64	3.8	316	0	0.0	1,360	64	4.7
1958	1,349	50	3.7	340	0	0.0	1,009	50	5.0
Baltimore									
1957	1,775	400	2.3	175	0	0.0	1,600	400	25.0
1958	1,900	524	2.8	320	NA	—	1,580	524	33.2
Cincinnati									
1957	1,350	243	18.0	235	0	0.0	1,115	243	21.8
1958	1,300	232	17.8	235	0	0.0	1,065	232	21.8
Dallas									
1957	1,961	160	8.2	NA	0	0.0	NA	160	—
1958	1,923	159	8.3	349	0	0.0	1,574	159	10.1
Detroit									
1957	9,066	NA	—	2,533	NA	—	6,533	NA	—
1958	7,222	247	3.4	2,294	0	0.0	4,231	247	5.8
Los Angeles									
1957	1,978	12	0.6	503	0	0.0	1,475	12	0.8
1958	1,490	40	2.7	278	0	0.0	1,212	40	3.3
Tarrytown, N.Y.									
1957	2,196	684	31.1	156	0	0.0	2,040	684	33.5
1958	2,056	671	32.6	156	1	0.6	1,900	670	35.3
7 Total[a]									
1957	20,002	1,563	14.3	3,918	0	0.0	14,123	1,563	18.5
1958	17,240	1,923	11.2	3,972	1	negligible	12,571	1,922	15.3
Kansas City									
1957	1,692	115	6.8	250	0	0.0	1,442	115	8.0
Linden, N.J.									
1957	3,700	578	15.6	583	0	0.0	3,117	578	18.5
St. Louis									
1957	2,800	250	8.9	400	0	0.0	1,400	250	17.9
San Francisco									
1957	1,260	223	17.7	195	0	0.0	1,065	223	20.9
11 Total									
1957	29,454	2,729	9.3	5,346	0	0.0	21,147	2,729	12.9

Source: Reports to the President's Committee on Government Contracts (Nixon Committee).

[a] The totals for *all* plants exclude only figures where *not available* (NA). The percent Negro figure is based on total employment and total Negro figures where *both* are given. For example, since the 1957 figure for total Negro employees in Detroit assembly is NA, the 9066 total Detroit employees are excluded from the 7 Total figure *when computing* percent Negro.

Note: There are obviously some small arithmetical errors in these data since they do not add up in both directions. These errors do not change the overall results.

One reason why General Motors has a smaller percentage of Negroes is because of the wide dispersion of its vast operations. General Motors has not only by far the most plants in the industry, but also many located in areas where few Negroes reside. In addition, General Motors is more diversified and product integrated than its two principal competitors, and some of its nonautomotive factories are less able than automotive plants to assimilate untrained labor.

Nevertheless, it is probably also true that General Motors adopted a fair employment program more slowly than did Ford or Chrysler and that it moved into affirmative action at a later date than did its competitors. As we shall see in the following section, General Motors is now firmly committed in this regard. General Motors also has moved vigorously on occasions in the past. It worked with the UAW to place Negroes in jobs other than laborers in Atlanta despite intense white employee opposition. It reacted strongly in overcoming local union leadership intimidation to accomplish the same in Kansas City. And it has operated under a strong policy on fair employment for many years. Yet it is the kind of company that moves slowly but surely. And its equal opportunity program reflects this managerial philosophy.

Table 7 shows the Negro employment in eleven General Motors plants in 1957 and 1958, as surveyed by a government procurement agency. These plants may not be representative. But they do illustrate the situation at General Motors plants in several parts of the country. For example, Negroes had sizable representation in the Cincinnati, Ohio, Tarrytown, New York, Linden, New Jersey, and San Francisco plants. Only at the New York plant, however, were Negroes represented among salaried employees—and there just one was colored.

The low representation among Negroes in General Motors Detroit facilities listed in Table 7 pertains to the Detroit Diesel plant. This operation, for reasons which are not clear, had a substantially smaller percentage of Negroes than did most General Motors facilities in either the Detroit area, or in other Michigan centers.

Among the plants in border state areas, Cincinnati had the highest percentage of Negroes, Baltimore, the lowest. Again, the reasons for these disparities are not known, but the vagaries of local managerial policies are probable answers. The 6.8 percent Negro employment in Kansas City marked considerable progress from prewar years. Negroes had once been confined to laborer and janitorial jobs there. When General Motors changed its policy after the War and offered production jobs to Negroes, the local union president allegedly visited each Negro employee and "advised" him not to seek an upgrade. Thus intimidated, no Negro employee would accept a promotion. General Motors broke this jam successfully by offering production jobs to Negro job applicants who were not then employees. When several new Negro employees accepted such jobs without incident, the Negro laborers and janitors asked for, and were granted, a new opportunity for upgrading.[29]

In the South, General Motors plants had a far higher percentage of Negroes than did Ford in this period. The percentage of Negroes at the Dallas (actually Arlington), Texas, plant was the highest of any automobile concern in the South. This plant was built after World War II and was not hindered by customs and practices of an earlier period.

General Motors, Atlanta operation, in which Negroes were much better represented than they were at Ford's in the same area, was nevertheless burdened with problems for both company and union. The union difficulties, already noted in the discussion of the World War II period, were commented upon by Professor Marshall as follows:

> . . . The UAW also has had considerable trouble . . . with its oldest Southern local in Atlanta [the G.M. local]. Indeed, this local even barred the eight Negro janitors in the plant from membership until forced by the international to admit them in 1946. Even after the Negroes were admitted, however, seating was segregated. In 1962 a Negro who attempted to sit in the white section was hit over the head with a chair by a white member. In 1961 Negroes were upgraded for the first time in the auto plant represented by this local. This gain for the Negroes was partly offset, however, by the loss of twelve jobs from which Negroes were "bumped" by whites after production lines were integrated.[30] [When employment increased later, these jobs were restored.]

Some local company officials, although certainly not violent, were equally devoted to the *status quo*. The *Wall Street Journal* in 1957 noting that the plant "employs only a few Negroes mainly for janitorial work," quoted the General Motors' Atlanta plant manager as saying:

29. Based on interviews by the author, November 1966.
30. Marshall, *The Negro and Organized Labor*, p. 179.

When we moved into the South, we agreed to abide by local custom and not hire Negroes for production work. This is no time for social reforming in that area and we're not about to try it.[31]

Obviously company policy was subject to considerable area influence even in the late 1950's. Yet despite this, General Motors, as noted, led Ford by a good margin in Negro employment in the South.

A strong factor in maintaining the *status quo* in southern plants at this time was the practice of hiring through state employment services. These agencies, although funded by the federal government, were highly segregated. The Negro sections often provided referrals to unskilled and service jobs only. Negroes in Atlanta, Dallas, or in other communities who wanted production or skilled work were referred to the state employment agencies by companies including automobile companies; but the Negro sections of these state agencies would neither test nor refer Negroes to the better jobs. Title VII of the Civil Rights Act of 1964 recognized this problem by forbidding such segregation on the part of federally supported state agencies.

THE RECESSION IMPACT, 1957-1960

As already indicated, the recession which began in late 1957, hit the automobile industry hard. Motor vehicle factory sales, which had soared to 9.2 million in 1955, a record not heretofore achieved nor surpassed for nine years, and which stood at 7.2 million in 1957, fell to 5.1 million in 1958. Ford employment dropped from 191,759 in 1957 to 142,076 in 1958; General Motors (world wide) from 588,160 to 520,625; and Chrysler, which already had a substantial number of employees on layoff, from 136,185 to 91,678. Negroes were heavily laid off, and in Detroit, as elsewhere, made up a disproportionate share of the unemployment. Detroit was designated by the federal government as a depressed area—that is, unemployment in excess of 6 percent of the labor force. In 1958, Detroit unemployment was estimated at 16.7 percent of the labor force; Negro unemployment at nearly twice this amount.[32] Since those on layoff had prior recall rights before new employees could be hired, it was

---

31. *Wall Street Journal*, October 24, 1957.
32. From reports of Michigan Unemployment Compensation Commission and Detroit Urban League.

in late 1962 or early 1963 before many plants in the industry again hired on the open market.

American Motors provided an exception to the industry's sales and employment problems. Capitalizing on the compact car, American consolidated its automotive operations in Kenosha and Milwaukee, Wisconsin, and proceeded to gain 7.2 percent of the new passenger car production in 1959 and 1960—the highest share of the market which American or its predecessor companies (Hudson and Nash) enjoyed since the war.

Negroes lost out when American closed the old Hudson Motor Car Company plants in Detroit between 1953 and 1957, for Negro employment at Hudson had averaged 10-15 percent of 25,330 production workers employed by that company in its postwar peak year of 1950. Employment did, however, steadily build up at American's Milwaukee and Kenosha plants, and the plants there which Dr. Bailer found employed no Negroes prior to World War II, had a Negro complement of about 8 percent of approximately 27,000 by 1960—nearly all in the basic production areas.[33]

Studebaker-Packard enjoyed no such resurgence in the late 1950's. Following the merger in 1954, this company's market share, which had stood at 6.5 percent in 1949 prior to the merger of the two companies, plunged steadily downward to 1.0 in 1958; it jumped back to 2.2 percent in 1959, but then declined until the company went out of the automobile business in the United States in December 1963, and in Canada, in March 1966.

Studebaker-Packard early in the merger abandoned the old Packard plants in Detroit, which even before World War II employed 600 Negroes out of a 16,000 labor force, and in which Negro employment stood at about 15 percent of the 16,818 in Packard's peak employment year of 1952.[34] In 1963, Studebaker also abandoned and sold off most of its South Bend, Indiana, works. This came at a time when employment was at peak levels in the South Bend area. Studebaker employed 26,696 workers in its peak premerger year of 1952; when it ceased production at South Bend, its force stood at 8,800, about 12 percent of whom were Negroes. Many of the former

---

33. Data estimated by author from various public and private sources.
34. For accounts of difficulties for Negro and white employees laid off by Packard in Detroit, see Michael Aiken and L. A. Ferman, "The Social and Political Reactions of Older Negroes to Unemployment," *Phylon*, Vol. XVII (Fourth Quarter 1966), pp. 333-346.

Studebaker Negro employees, having less seniority, had been laid off before the company gave up automobile production in South Bend.[35] Said Studebaker's Director of Personnel in December 1967:

> Since our cessation of automobile production . . . we have done no hiring in South Bend. At that time, we had Negro personnel in our employment office, a Negro Supervisor of Industrial Relations, a draftsman, two secretaries, and a percentage in the factory well above the population ratio in the South Bend area. Due to a constant reduction in force, all have been laid off . . . only one Negro remains in the union because of his seniority.[36]

Despite the setbacks of the recession and plant closings, Negro employment in the industry experienced a definite upward trend in the 1950's, as in previous decades. Table 8 shows the decennial census reports since 1930 for Standard Industrial Classification 371—Motor Vehicles and Equipment. By 1960, nonwhites (nearly all Negro) comprised 9.1 percent of the labor force attached to that part of the industry included in the census version of SIC 371, as compared with 7.8 percent in 1950 and 3.7 percent in 1940. The greatest employment gains of Negroes were made during the World War II period. In the decade of the 1950's Negroes did slightly better than hold their own, but in view of the plant closings in the middle of the 1950's and the severe recession of 1958, these data make it obvious that Negro workers were a significant and permanent sector of the industry's work force by 1960 which would not be dislodged by economic misfortune.

The Negro automobile labor force in 1960 was, however, confined almost exclusively to production jobs. As late as 1962, Negroes comprised less than one percent of the white collar and professional employment and barely one-half of one percent of the skilled craftsmen in one of the Big Three companies; another had no nonwhite clerical employees throughout most of the 1950's; and the third made little progress in this area. Gains in these job categories would have to wait until the 1960's.

---

35. For the experiences in placing the older Studebaker employees, see *Project Able*, Final Report, Contract No. MDS 37-64, Older Worker Employment, United Community Services of St. Joseph County, Inc., 1965; and J. John Paley and Frank J. Paley, "Unemployment and Reemployment Success: An Analysis of the Studebaker Shutdown," *Industrial and Labor Relations Review*, Vol. XXI (January 1958), pp. 234-250.
36. *A Current Look At: (1) The Negro and Title VII, (2) Sex and Title VII*, Washington: Bureau of National Affairs, Inc., 1967, Personnel Policies Forum, Survey No. 82, p. 6.

TABLE 8.   *Total Employed Persons by Race and Sex for Motor Vehicles and Motor Vehicle Equipment, 1930-1960*
(SIC 371)[a]

Year	All Employees Total	All Employees Male	All Employees Female	Nonwhite Employees[b] Total	Nonwhite Employees[b] Male	Nonwhite Employees[b] Female	Percent Nonwhite Employees Total	Percent Nonwhite Employees Male	Percent Nonwhite Employees Female
1930[c]	640,474	595,433	45,041	29,834	29,504	330	4.7	5.0	0.7
1940	574,931	525,010	49,921	21,005	20,794	211	3.7	4.0	0.4
1950	868,974	759,545	109,429	67,885	63,572	4,313	7.8	8.4	3.9
1960	836,681	745,260	91,421	76,296	71,594	4,702	9.1	9.6	5.1

[a] Comparability: 1930 category "Automobile Factories," 1940 category "Automobiles and Automobile Equipment," and 1950, 1960 category "Motor Vehicles and Motor Vehicle Equipment" appear to be comparable. These categories include firms which do one of the following: (a) assemble or manufacture completed autos, trucks, and buses; (b) manufacture truck or auto bodies; (c) manufacture automobile parts and accessories.

[b] Nonwhite includes very small numbers of Orientals and American Indians.

[c] 1930 census compiled employment data differently than did later censuses. 1930 collected data on "gainful workers" which, unlike later censuses, did not distinguish between persons employed and persons unemployed but seeking work. The inclusion of the latter category tends to inflate employment statistics for a given industry. Also 1930 census includes workers 10 years and older; 1940-1960, 14 years and older.

Source: U. S. Census of Population:
        1960: PC (2)7A, *Occupational Characteristics,* Table 37.
        1950: Vol. II, *Characteristics of the Population,* Part 1, *United States Summary,* Table 133.
        1940: Vol. III, *The Labor Force,* Table 76.
        1930: Vol. V, *General Report on Occupations,* Table 2, p. 468.

CHAPTER VI.

Industrial Expansion and Civil Rights
1960-1967

The rise in civil rights emphasis in the 1960's, by a happy coincidence, came at a time of great prosperity in the automobile industry. Moreover, it happened when a natural turnover was occurring in the industry. Many employees hired around World War II, or earlier, were seeking retirement under the liberalized early, and regular retirement programs in the industry. Between 1962 and 1967, the United Automobile Workers took in 842,000 new workers—more than one-half of its total membership.[37] The need for Negroes to obtain jobs and the need of an industry for new workers were never better coordinated.

RECESSION AND PROSPERITY

The decade of the 1960's did not commence so propitiously. Although 1960 was a fairly good sales year for the industry, it was below the previous decade peak year of 1955. Then came another downturn in 1961, in which Chrysler was hit especially hard by lack of sales. But thereafter, sales rose, and as Table 9 shows, employment followed suit, with one record year following another through 1965, and with 1966 second only to 1965 in unit sales.

As already noted, the Big Three companies began the decade of the 1960's with substantial layoff lists, dating back to the 1958 recession mainly, but Chrysler in many cases to the early 1950's. The recession of 1961, following on the heels of the more severe one of 1958, forced such cutbacks that in some plants it required twenty-five years seniority to hold a job. Chrysler was forced to lay off 49,000 employees, including 7,000 white collar ones, because of the sales decline and the need to reduce costs in 1961. Thereafter,

---

37. *Wall Street Journal*, July 6, 1967, p. 1.

TABLE 9. *Domestic Employment, Big Three Automobile Companies, 1960-1966*

| Year | Company | | | Total Three Companies |
	General Motors	Ford	Chrysler	
1960	457,965	160,181	105,410	723,556
1961	464,150	154,659	74,377	693,186
1962	486,869	186,640	77,194	750,703
1963	499,818	187,428	90,752	777,998
1964	545,347	197,578	104,845	847,770
1965	580,451	217,741	126,000	924,192
1966	586,622	233,849	133,114	953,585

Source: Company annual reports. Ford data excludes Philco-Ford and other subsidiary companies; General Motors and Chrysler data include nonautomotive operations such as appliances, locomotives, and aerospace products.

however, Chrysler surged forward to regain much of its market position, and eventually to expand employment well beyond 1960 levels, but so far, not up to the peak years of the 1950's.

The prosperity of the 1960's was not shared by the independents. As already noted, Studebaker went out of the business altogether. From a share of 7.2 percent in 1960, American Motors lost position slowly for three years, and then more rapidly until by 1966 it held only 2.5 percent of the market. Negro employment in its Milwaukee and Kenosha plants dropped at least proportionately, remaining at approximately 8 percent, while total employment in these plants dipped from a peak of approximately 27,000 in 1960 to less than 18,000 in 1966.

NEGRO EMPLOYMENT IN THE 1960's— THE GENERAL PICTURE

There is no doubt that Negroes were the biggest gainers as employment rose in the 1960's following the surge in automobile sales. From a depressed area with a labor surplus and unemployment in excess of 16 percent, Detroit turned into a highly prosperous one, importing workers to overcome a critical labor shortage. Anyone willing and able to work could find it—and with earnings which in 1966 averaged about $150 per week.

At the same time that sales and employment began to rise, greater emphasis on the need for Negro employment commenced. The Kennedy Administration reorganized and greatly strengthened the equal opportunity work done by the procurement agencies and the President's Committee on Equal Employment Opportunity (now the Office of Federal Contract Compliance). In addition, major corporations, including the Big Three automobile companies, were invited to join the Plans for Progress Program, in which the companies pledge themselves to work actively and affirmatively to further minority group employment.

Once the laid off workers of the 1950's and the 1961 recession were recalled, the Big Three automobile companies had little difficulty living up to their Plans for Progress pledges insofar as production workers in the northern industrial centers were concerned. The Detroit area, in particular, saw Negroes emerge as the dominant group in production in many plants. A tour of blue collar employment offices in Detroit any time since 1965 would reveal very few white applicants except at the time of school closings, or summer vacation, or unless the applicant was qualified for a skilled trade. In other parts of the country also Negro employment in the industry rose faster than total employment.

Table 10 shows the number and percentage of Negroes by occupational groupings for the Big Three companies. Negroes made up 13.6 percent of the labor force of the Big Three by the end of 1966, a percentage slightly larger than their ratio in the general population. In production operations, Negroes comprised about 25 percent of the work force—more than twice the percentage of Negroes to whites in the total labor force. In production operations, Negroes are, moreover, not confined to any particular type jobs or departments. Although they are slightly more concentrated in service and laborers jobs than as operatives, the difference in job rates or types of jobs among these groups is not great. Negroes work side by side with whites on all jobs in assembly plants, stamping and other manufacturing plants, and in all types of jobs associated with production in these areas. It is doubtful if Negroes have so large a share of production jobs in any other major industry.

TABLE 10. *Total and Negro Employment for Combined Big Three Automobile Companies, 1966*

	All Employees			Male Employees			Female Employees		
	Total	Negro	Percent Negro	Total	Negro	Percent Negro	Total	Negro	Percent Negro
Officials and Managers	74,395	903	1.2	74,061	903	1.2	334	0	0.0
Professionals	51,053	301	0.6	50,380	287	0.6	673	14	0.2
Technicians	24,499	297	1.2	23,316	268	1.1	1,183	29	2.5
Sales, Office, and Clerical	93,365	3,545	3.8	57,650	2,768	4.8	35,715	777	2.2
Craftsmen	129,123	3,846	3.0	129,042	3,842	3.0	81	4	4.9
Operatives	515,843	104,112	20.2	460,702	98,313	21.3	55,141	5,799	10.5
Laborers	32,352	8,922	27.6	31,649	8,826	27.9	703	96	13.7
Service Workers	26,755	7,269	27.2	24,898	6,855	27.5	1,857	414	22.3
Total	947,385	129,195	13.6	851,698	122,062	14.3	95,687	7,133	7.5

Source: Data in author's possession.

THE CRAFTSMEN PROBLEM

Insofar as craftsmen are concerned, the situation is quite different. In 1966, Negroes comprised only 3 percent of the 129,123 skilled personnel in this group in Big Three plants. Despite a shortage of craftsmen and energetic efforts on the part of the companies to recruit personnel, this situation has been difficult to change for several reasons.

Traditionally, skilled craftsmen in the automobile industry have come from three sources: company apprentice programs; employment of those who learned their skills elsewhere, including immigrants; and upgraders or learners trained on the job after production experience.

The apprentice programs have always attracted a high type person —the high school graduate with good mechanical and mathematical aptitude who did not make it to college because of family attitudes or finances. They have traditionally been the "middle class" of automobile workers—a white elite who did not associate with the producation men.[38] Like building tradesmen, the skilled trades group have been antagonistic toward accepting Negroes into their group. Moreover, supervisory personnel in the skilled trades area have traditionally come up through the ranks, and undoubtedly share the general attitudes attributed to the rank and file. As will be discussed below, the UAW does not seem to have made great progress in changing attitudes or policies among the skilled trades.[39]

Since, with rare exceptions, only Ford accepted Negroes as apprentices prior to World War II, and since progress made by the industry prior to 1960 in attracting Negro apprentices was rather limited, the exclusionist attitudes of the skilled trades groups have been reinforced by industry experience. Historically, most Negroes have come to regard all apprenticeship programs as closed to them. There is little reason to believe that this feeling has been substantially overcome in the automobile industry.

Now that the automobile companies have not only opened their ranks to Negroes, but have been eagerly seeking apprentice candidates, other factors mitigate against success for Negroes in these jobs.

---

38. For a good discussion of the social and ethnic backgrounds of the craftsmen, which tend to separate them from the production personnel, see Stanley H. Brown, "Walter Reuther: 'He's Got to Walk That Last Mile,'" *Fortune,* Vol. LXXVI (July 1967), pp. 89, 141-142.

39. Marshall, *The Negro and Organized Labor,* pp. 68-69.

Negroes who apply find that they are less proficient in mathematics and score lower as a group in tests than do whites. Most of the Negroes applying come either from southern segregated institutions or from less desirable areas of the cities. In either case, their training is likely to compare unfavorably with that of whites from better surroundings. For example, in a sampling of applicants of one company in early 1967, only four Negroes of a total of 267 who took the preapprentice admission test passed the mathematics examination. Moreover, these four had scores that were marginal and therefore, in competition for openings in the apprentice program, were unlikely to gain admittance. Whenever apprentice openings occur, it has been the policy in at least one company to select those with the highest scores regardless of when the test was taken. Hence low scores may never be admitted. (The companies are limited by union contract on the number of apprentices in relation to journeymen whom they may employ. The General Motors contract, for example, limits the apprentice ratio to one per eight journeymen in a given craft. The contract permits flexibility, however, depending on the local area and/or craft skill supply and demand situation. Ratios as low as one for one have been negotiated for recent periods.)

The failure of Negroes to qualify for apprenticeship programs is a persistent problem. The same company from which the test score sample was taken now finds about 25 percent of its applicants for apprenticeship are Negroes, but only about 12 percent of those qualifying are Negroes. Moreover, those qualifying are on the low side. They find openings in apprentice classes for millwrights, pipe fitters, and welders. The tool and die and electrical trades take those with the highest scores, and few Negroes now make up these groups or qualify for them.

Tests, of course, are not identical among the three companies, and are never the only criteria for determining acceptance into apprenticeship programs. Tests are designed to determine whether the applicant is capable of handling high school mathematics, a prerequisite for comprehension of shop mathematics. The Ford program requires that an applicant be 18-27 years of age, have a tenth grade education, with a C average, and a successful joint union-management interview. The General Motors rules require that applicants be 18-26 years of age, and be a high school graduate or have equivalent education. General Motors neither requires nor suggests a joint union-management interview. The key elements, in all cases, are mathematical aptitude and comprehension, and a high school education. Those who score high in the premployment tests are eagerly sought after and readily accepted.

Most Negroes who now meet these criteria, like most whites, go to college instead of into an apprentice program. Since proportionately fewer Negroes are available, their disproportionate showing among the apprentice applicants is likely to continue.

Ford and the UAW agreed in the 1967 negotiations to an experiment to try and break the testing cycle which has kept Negro representation in the apprentice program so low. Forty colored and forty white low scorers—that is, those who passed the tests, but with marginal performances—were accepted into the apprentice program ahead of high scorers. Their progress will be watched carefully to determine whether low scorers can become satisfactory apprentices and craftsmen, and therefore whether the tests need restructuring or reinterpreting. Ford is also having its tests thoroughly re-examined and restudied to determine whether built-in bias is influencing results.

Company apprenticeship programs in the automobile industry are not limited to new or to youthful applicants. For example, at General Motors, for those already on the company rolls, the age requirement is greatly expanded. General Motors will accept into the apprenticeship program employees in the 27-40 age group. Where qualifications "of the employe-applicant and non-employe-applicant are equal, the employe-applicant will be given preference." The General Motors agreement with the UAW also provides that "For all applicants placed on apprentice training in any given year, the ratio of those in the 27-40 age group to those under 27 years of age shall in no event exceed one to two in the particular trade involved."

Employees who demonstrate competence can be given credit for previous experience and can thus shorten the four-year apprentice training period and also receive wage rate adjustments. Employees transferred into apprentice training continue to accumulate seniority in the seniority group from which they transfer, as well as begin to accumulate seniority as an apprentice in a particular craft.

Applicants for apprentice training among Negro employees have always been markedly less than their proportion in the work force. There are several reasons for this. The first, of course, is that Negroes are less well educated and more likely to be deficient in mathematical comprehension and general educational requirements. Moreover, these jobs have traditionally been closed to Negroes—except at Ford's River Rouge plant and a few others. To apply for apprentice training has been to "go out of bounds," as a Negro assembly line worker told the author.[40] Now that such job training is available, past practices and customs are difficult to overcome. The fact that so few Negroes are in the skilled crafts, discourages others from trying. It is more compatible to be where fellow members of one's race are clearly accepted and already found in large numbers.

Because of the high pay of production workers, a temporary sacrifice in earnings is likely to be required to enter the apprentice training program. This demands both a long-run view, strong motivation, and confidence in the future. Such apprentice candidates do not sacrifice their seniority, but apparently this is not enough motivation. Discrimination and motivation go hand in hand. Because of the pervasiveness of the former in the life of Negroes, the latter is often lacking. Opportunities for training which require sacrifice for eventual improvement are not grasped. Inexperience in industry, lack of family help in setting goals, the absence of similar opportunities in previous generations, and the difficulty of breaking with the past all continue to reduce the number of Negroes who grasp the opportunities for skilled trades training.

It is expecting much to believe that Negroes will take advantage of such training opportunities without special effort. If the number of Negro apprentices applying from existing employees is to be increased, it appears obvious that special motivational and training efforts will have to be made. Educational and motivational deficiencies must be overcome if qualifications are to be raised and if the desire is to be created to acquire the skills which both pay very well and provide a trade that will likely always be useful. There have been efforts to encourage Negro employees to go into the apprentice programs, but they have been neither massive nor particularly successful thus far. Whether with greater effort on the part of the companies, greater success would result cannot be predicted, but such efforts would at least provide the answer for the industry and its critics.

Negroes are largely unrepresented among those craftsmen who enter the automobile industry after training in other industries or countries. Detroit's skilled craftsmen have always included a sizable number trained abroad, including many who make their way from the metals industries of Europe and Britain, through Canada, or directly. The high wages also attract craftsmen from other industries.

---

40. Interview, eastern automobile plant, November 1967.

Since few industries have been as willing to hire Negroes as has the automobile industry, and since no Negroes are found among the skilled immigrants, these recruits to the industry are virtually all white.

Upgraders or learners represent the most likely source of skilled Negro craftsmen for the future. They are production workers who are given training, first as helpers, and then as skilled workers, and thus learn a trade without a formal apprenticeship program, and without sacrificing their pay scale. In the past, both companies and the UAW Skilled Trades Department have been accused of reluctance to open up opportunities to Negroes.[41] This is certainly no longer so, but again the problem of background and education limits the number of Negroes who can handle these skills. In addition, companies cite a discouraging number of cases in which Negroes with requisite backgrounds preferred to stay on production jobs and not take the necessary training. Given, however, the tremendous size of the Negro labor force in the industry, it is likely that a slow but steady increase in their representation among skilled craftsmen should result *via* the upgrading route. Progress is likely to be slow because, again, of the educational, motivational, and in a steadily declining proportion, discriminatory barriers. The expanding Negro production labor force, however, would seem to insure an increasing spillover into skilled trade upgrading promotions, and it is likely that affirmative action on the part of the companies to expand their Negro skilled trades force will somewhat accelerate the pace.

MANAGERS, PROFESSIONALS, AND TECHNICAL EMPLOYEES

Progress in the salaried area has been slow, but since 1962 the major companies have been making a determined effort to recruit Negro professionals, technicians, and office workers. There are a limited number of Negroes with sufficient training for professional and technical jobs and not only automobile companies, but in fact companies in almost every major industry are attempting to recruit them. Consequently, the number of Negroes in these jobs is certain to rise but to increase slowly.

A number of changes have occurred in company policy in regard to professional and technical personnel. Most noteworthy is the decision of General Motors to open the General Motors Institute to

---

41. Marshall, *supra*, note 39.

Negroes, and to recruit Negroes intensively to attend the Institute. The General Motors Institute is an accredited five-year college at Flint, Michigan, which is a training ground for future General Motors executives. In 1967, the company reported that there were 18 Negroes among the 3,000 students, and that for the first time Negroes in 1967 would be in the graduating class.[42]

In the officials and managers group are included supervisory personnel. Most Negroes in this group are line supervisors or foremen, but a few have made it farther up the ladder. Negroes are beginning to appear in personnel and other staff positions, in accounting departments, and less frequently in line operations above the general foreman classification. Again progress is likely to be slow because of the few Negroes who are qualified for higher management jobs, the intense competition among various industries and companies to recruit qualified Negroes, and the equally intense internal competition in the automobile companies for managerial positions which offer rich pecuniary and status rewards.

DEALERS AND SALESMEN

Automobile companies do not have sales personnel in the traditional sense. Salesmen work for dealers who are independent businessmen operating company-awarded franchises. For many years, Edward B. Davis, a Detroit Negro, was the only Negro franchised dealer. He held a Studebaker franchise for 17 years, and then in 1962, became a Chrysler dealer.[43] Not until 1967, did Ford and General Motors announce the awarding of dealerships to Negroes.

Having so few Negroes among the nearly 29,000 franchised dealers in domestic automobiles is scarcely an outstanding record. The companies point out that they have had great difficulty in finding a Negro entrepreneur with the requisite business background, ability, who has also the necessary access to capital and credit resources. "The companies insist that they are not discriminatory and would be willing to sign up Negroes who know the auto business and have the financial backing necessary."[44]

Merely desiring to have a Negro dealer, and waiting for one to

---

42. *New York Times,* July 16, 1967, p. 53.
43. *Detroit News,* August 31, 1967; *Detroit Free Press,* September 1, 1967; and *New York Times,* September 2, 1967.
44. *Ibid.*

come along, proved insufficient. In August 1957, Mr. Virgil E. Boyd, president of Chrysler, announced a program of direct recruitment and training designed to set up in business Negroes who want to be car dealers as "the only way to get these people placed." Mr. Boyd's program calls for recruiting prospects from among "several hundred Negroes who now hold jobs as salesmen or sales managers in white-owned dealerships. . . . "[45]

Chrysler started a program several years ago when Mr. Boyd was sales vice-president to expand Negro representation among the sales force of the company and its dealers. The number of Negroes in these groups rose from 11 to 400 in two years. According to Mr. Boyd, a number of Negro salesmen have progressed to sales manager positions. They and other candidates are being considered for the Chrysler Institute, a special six-months course in dealer business operations, which traditionally has been operated as a training course for sons of Chrysler dealers. After six months at the Institute, trainees are given field instruction at dealerships. Negro candidates will train at both the Davis dealership and at white-owned dealerships. The first Negro graduate of the Institute, Donald Thomas, entered after working in Chrysler's personnel department. Prospective dealers, once trained, will be backed financially by the company if they can "come up with a nominal investment."[46]

Although all companies are, as Mr. Davis, the pioneer Negro automobile dealer, has stated, "now earnestly trying to get qualified men as dealers" without discrimination, it undoubtedly will require a program like Chrysler's to achieve solid results. Ford has established a similar program. Developments like the Chrysler plan, which commenced with six candidates at one time, will not show dramatic results for a number of years. The opportunities are there, and, as Chrysler has recognized, successful Negro dealers in many metropolitan areas which have sizeable Negro population, are certain both to attract business and to provide leadership and inspiration for Negroes interested in business opportunities.

Chrysler's program should also have salutory results on Negro representation among regional officers and dealer salesmen. As already noted, Chrysler has already moved to strengthen Negro representation in these areas. The other companies have likewise done so. All the Big Three have successfully encouraged and assisted dealers

45. *Ibid.*
46. *Ibid.*

in recruiting Negro salesmen, particularly in the large cities where Negro population is now a significant sources of sales. No data are available on the number or percentage of Negro salesmen other than the Chrysler figures already cited, but the author has found them with increasing frequency in big city dealerships in the East and Midwest.

On the other hand, regional and district offices typically have few Negroes. The industry does not list such regional and district personnel as salesmen, for they do not sell to the consumer. They aid and oversee dealers, handle customer and public relations problems, and generally look out for the interests of the companies. This is an area in which Negroes in nearly every industry are poorly represented, and the automobile industry is no significant exception.

OFFICE AND CLERICAL

In the office and clerical group, the fact that Negroes represent only 4 percent of the total indicates the late start in hiring such Negro personnel, the progress during the 1960's when the bulk of the 3,500 Negroes were employed in offices, and certain locational difficulties. Because of its late start in employing Negroes in clerical and white collar jobs, the industry must now compete for a scarce supply of qualified personnel. Moreover, employment habits have been slow to change, despite changes in company policies. Given the greater training of whites and the superiority of the schools which they are likely to attend, special programs and training are likely to be required to increase substantially Negro participation in clerical and office jobs. Since, in addition, turnover in accounting, sales office, and other jobs is not high among male office and clerical employees, the representation of Negroes is not likely to increase rapidly.

As we shall note below in our discussion of regional and locational difficulties, where plants and offices are located in suburbs or in other areas outside of Detroit where Negroes cannot find housing, Negro males are willing to commute long distances, but females are not. Like most women who have households to care for, Negro females want work close to home. The general offices of Chrysler and General Motors are located in the heart of the Detroit area; Ford is at Dearborn, an outlying area; and many plant locations and their offices are farther out of Detroit or other metropolitan areas. Where potential Negro clerical help cannot live close by, it is difficult to obtain.

REGIONAL AND LOCATIONAL FACTORS

Developments in the 1960's have varied by region and by company, as they have in the past. Detroit in particular, and Michigan in general, continue to have the highest concentration of Negroes in the industry. Like many northern industrial centers, Detroit has had a heavy inmigration of Negroes, and an even heavier outmigration of whites. The Negro percentage of the population in other Michigan automotive centers is also substantial. The estimated ratio of Negro population for Detroit in 1965 was 39 percent; of Flint, 22 percent; Grand Rapids, 11 percent; Pontiac, 21 percent; and Saginaw, 24 percent. Projections for these areas indicate a continued rise in the ratio of Negroes to whites, with Detroit expected to be about 50 percent Negro by 1970.[47]

Negro representation in production operations has more than kept pace with the Negro population growth in the greater Detroit area. Some downtown Chrysler plants, for example, have a majority of Negro hourly employees; on the second shift (shift preference is by seniority), the ratio has been as high as 85 percent Negro. The Ford River Rouge works is about 37 percent Negro in total and 46 percent Negro in the production areas. Plants with 30 to 50 percent Negro are quite common throughout the Greater Detroit area.[48]

An interesting aspect of Detroit area Negro automobile employment is the relatively high percentage in suburban areas where housing is completely closed to Negroes. An assembly plant, for example, twenty miles from center city, which can be reached only by car traveling on a turnpike that bisects several all-white communities, is 26 percent Negro. A prime reason is that employees who once worked closer to midtown Detroit transferred with their work when the new suburban assembly plant was built, and the plant became known as a place where Negroes were well received.

Where new plants have been built in the suburbs, Negroes have found work there despite the absence of housing open to them. For example, in a new stamping plant, which is also located in a sub-

---

47. Data from U. S. Census. See also *The Negro Population: 1965 Estimates and 1970 Projections* (Peekskill, N. Y.: The Center for Research in Marketing, Inc., February 1966).
48. All data are the author's estimates based on information in his possession.

urban area, 18 percent of the labor force is Negro. The absence of housing for Negroes in such areas, however, insures that very few Negro females will be employed in such plants.

Seniority provisions have been of considerable aid in helping Negroes find work throughout the Detroit area, or in other areas where a number of plants of one company are located. When openings occur, the Chrysler agreement, for example, provides that preference be given, first, to qualified laid off employees of other departments in the plant, and second, to such employees who have been laid off by other Chrysler plants in the area. Employees do not lose their seniority if they refuse such job offers, but they then cannot collect supplemental unemployment benefits. With such provisions, it is not possible to confine Negroes to particular departments or plants because in effect a general labor pool is created, which has first chance at openings at any area plant or department covered by the agreement.

Like Ford and Chrysler, General Motors has a high concentration of Negro production workers in the greater Detroit area, where 25 to 45 percent of its employees in these categories are Negro. In Flint, Pontiac, Lansing, Grand Rapids, and Saginaw, General Motors plants with 15-25 percent Negro employment, or occasionally even higher, are typical.

In other eastern and midwestern cities, the percentage of Negroes in assembly and manufacturing plants varies considerably. Chicago plants range from 13 to 30 percent Negro; Cleveland plants from 13 to 21 percent; and those in the New York City area, from 12 to 30 percent. In areas where few Negroes reside, for example, Wisconsin, very few are found in automotive plants. Except in the New York area, where housing nearby outlying plants is available to Negroes, plants in suburban areas do not have a high Negro complement as they do in Detroit. The sight of Negroes traveling toward, and working in automobile plants, far out of center city, and far from Negro housing opportunities, is much more common in Detroit than elsewhere.

In California plants, Negroes comprised 12.8 percent of the Big Three total employment, 17.2 of the operatives, but, as usual, substantially smaller percentages of the craftsmen and salaried personnel. These data are found in Table 11. Although California was estimated to have only a 6 percent Negro population in 1965, Los Angeles was estimated at 18 percent, Oakland at 31 percent, San Francisco

TABLE 11. *Total and Negro Employment for Big Three West Coast Plants, 1966*

	All Employees			Male Employees			Female Employees		
	Total	Negro	Percent Negro	Total	Negro	Percent Negro	Total	Negro	Percent Negro
Officials and Managers	2,036	35	1.7	2,036	35	1.7	0	0	0.0
Professionals	765	4	0.5	748	4	0.5	17	0	0.0
Technicians	341	7	2.1	308	7	2.3	33	0	0.0
Sales, Office, and Clerical	3,168	183	5.8	2,325	177	7.6	843	6	0.7
Craftsmen	1,518	39	2.6	1,518	39	2.6	0	0	0.0
Operatives	15,929	2,739	17.2	15,891	2,739	17.2	38	0	0.0
Laborers	1,186	159	13.4	1,180	158	13.4	6	1	16.7
Service Workers	841	137	16.3	841	137	16.3	0	0	0.0
Total	25,784	3,303	12.8	24,847	3,296	13.3	937	7	0.7

Source: Data in author's possession.

TABLE 12. *Total and Negro Employment for Southern Plants of General Motors and Ford, 1966*

	All Employees			Male Employees			Female Employees		
	Total	Negro	Percent Negro	Total	Negro	Percent Negro	Total	Negro	Percent Negro
Officials and Managers	3,512	28	0.8	3,511	28	0.8	1	0	0.0
Professionals	1,280	8	0.6	1,263	7	0.6	17	1	5.9
Technicians	260	7	2.7	220	6	2.7	40	1	2.5
Sales, Office, and Clerical	5,798	166	2.9	4,702	155	3.3	1,096	11	1.0
Craftsmen	2,786	12	0.4	2,786	12	0.4	0	0	0.0
Operatives	26,008	3,232	12.4	25,983	3,231	12.4	25	1	4.0
Laborers	2,992	447	15.0	2,990	447	15.0	2	0	0.0
Service Workers	1,470	359	24.4	1,469	358	24.4	1	1	100.0
Total	44,106	4,259	9.7	42,924	4,244	9.9	1,182	15	1.3

Source: Data in author's possession.

at 14 percent.[49] Since most automobile plants are in or nearby these cities, Negro representation in these areas has about kept pace with the population.

In border cities, such as Wilmington, Delaware, Baltimore, St. Louis, Kansas City, Cincinnati, and Louisville, Negro employment varies considerably, with the percentage of production employees anywhere from 4 to 17 percent, but with very few Negro white collar employees or craftsmen. The Indianapolis area plants follow a similar pattern. Automobile plants located in smaller Ohio, Illinois, or Indiana communities do not generally employ a high percentage of Negroes, particularly if they are on the southern borders of these states.

The situation in the South is the weakest in terms of Negro employment. Table 12 shows that less than 10 percent of the total employment in southern automobile plants in 1966 was Negro, with heavy concentration in the lowest job brackets. These plants were generally operated on a strictly segregated basis until 1961, with separate seniority lines in some cases that confined Negroes to the service and laboring jobs. The pioneering which Henry Ford did at River Rouge was not repeated by Ford or his successors in the South. Nor did General Motors fill the breach, and Chrysler has no southern automotive plants.

The UAW likewise, as we have already noted, has not been much of a pioneer in southern automotive plants. In contrast to the record of both companies and the union in the automotive plants at Atlanta, Norfolk, and Dallas, have been the efforts of the International Harvester Company and the same UAW in Memphis, Tennessee and at other locations. International Harvester abolished separate facilities and integrated the work force in southern plants in the immediate post-World War II period, and the UAW put a rebellious local in trusteeship when it attempted to challenge that company's racial policies.[50]

In contrast, Ford and General Motors were slow to buck southern custom. Apparently, they feared a white reaction which might have

---

49. See note 47 for sources.

50. On the International Harvester experience, see John Hope II, *Negro Employment in 3 Southern Plants of International Harvester Company* (Washington, D. C.: National Planning Association, 1953), Committee of the South Report No. 6; Robert Ozanne, *A Century of Labor Management Relations at McCormick and International Harvester* (Madison, Wis.: University of Wisconsin Press, 1967), pp. 183-193; and Marshall, *op. cit.*, pp. 178-179.

harmed sales. Yet if *both* had moved, it is unlikely that customer reaction could have damaged *both* companies, especially since Chrysler, the main alternative for the consumer, remained the employer with the largest proportion of Negroes in its work force. Finally in 1961 the companies, with UAW cooperation, put an end to sanctioned discrimination and segregation. Progress in upgrading and hiring has followed, but has been slowed, especially in the Ford plants, because some of the facilities have had only limited expansion and relatively small turnover.

COMPANY DIFFERENCES

Chrysler continues to lead in the ratio of Negroes employed. Again a principal reason appears to be locational, since Chrysler remains the most concentrated in the central Detroit area, and has no plants in the South where equal employment opportunity in the industry has progressed the least, and very few plants in areas where Negro population is a very small ratio. In 1966, 23.1 percent of Chrysler's total work force and about 30 percent of its production workers were Negroes.[51]

Chrysler's favorable position in regard to Negroes is bolstered by a very strong managerial attitude. Company officials, starting with the Chief Executive, have made the Company's position very clear. It has been in the forefront on a variety of special training projects such as the already noted one for potential Negro dealers, which are designed to improve Negro educational opportunities and to open up new vistas for Negroes. Its border city plants in Delaware and St. Louis have a substantially higher percentage of Negro employees than do comparable plants of other companies. And like its two bigger competitors, it strives hard to recruit Negroes for its managerial, professional, and technical positions.

Chrysler also leads its competitors in the percentage of Negro officials and managers. Nearly 3 percent of this important category at Chrysler are Negro. Most of those in this category are supervisors and foremen, but some higher rated officials and staff members are involved. With its high percentage of Negroes, Chrysler has had, and accepted, the opportunity to upgrade Negroes to supervisory positions

---

51. All data in this section, unless otherwise noted, are the author's estimates based upon data in his possession.

with considerable success. In all three companies, Negro foremen supervised mixed crews.

At the professional and technical levels, Chrysler is also slightly ahead of its competitors, but the percentage differences among the three companies are too small to be significant. All three companies, as noted, are, with most other large concerns, avidly recruiting eligible Negroes in these categories, but the very small number of qualified Negroes, particularly in engineering, is a major obstacle to overcome.

Chrysler's marketing policies, including its pioneering with the first Negro dealer, and with the program to increase dealer opportunities for Negroes, go hand in hand with its employment policies. Advertising in the Negro press and to the Negro communities not only attempts to capitalize on its employment policies, but further stresses the record of Chrysler as an equal opportunity employer, and probably the company with the highest ratio of Negro employees among major American Corporations.

Ford's total Negro employment ratio in 1966 was 15.9 percent, with nearly 22 percent of its production workers Negro. As already noted, the huge River Rouge complex has a substantially higher Negro proportion.

Ford leads the industry in both the skilled craftsmen and office and clerical ratio of Negroes. In 1966, nearly 6 percent of Ford's skilled craftsmen and nearly 7 percent of its office and clerical workers were Negro. The historic willingness of Ford to utilize Negroes in all skills, and the fact that it has been well-known in the Detroit Negro community for several generations, that Ford accepts applications for its apprenticeship program from Negroes, undoubtedly go far to explain Ford's superior progress in this category.

Ford's top showing in the office and clerical field is of particular interest because its headquarters is farther from the center of Detroit's Negro population than are either General Motors' or Chrysler's. One reason is the large representation of Negroes in the plant offices in Chicago and New Jersey, as already noted in Table 6. Another is the traditional appeal of Ford to Negroes which aids in recruiting. And a third is the sincere effort in recent years of Ford officials to increase Negro representation in all salaried positions.

In 1966, General Motors employed 56,762 Negroes in the United States—probably the largest number employed by any company but a smaller percentage—9.8—than either of its major competitors. We have already noted several reasons for General Motors ratio lag.

For one thing, General Motors is less concentrated in the Detroit area, and has numerous plants in areas where few Negroes live. In addition, General Motors' many plants in nonautomotive products include operations with a higher overall skill content than do basic automotive plants. In view of the disproportionate lack of skills among Negroes, this, of course, hinders their employment.

General Motors maintains a tremendous number of offices in cities throughout the country in order to care for its various business activities. Slowness in recruiting Negroes for regional sales work and for office and clerical jobs in general, and difficulties in finding qualified personnel in recent years are significant factors in holding down General Motors' proportion of Negroes.

A historic problem for General Motors was the reluctance of some decentralized managers to give effect to equal employment opportunity. The Corporation then adopted a strong policy which reduced local managerial discretion in this regard, and then brought it under even stricter central office control. Progress in the 1960's has been noteworthy. For example, in 1963, General Motors' domestic employment increased 2.7 percent over the previous year, but nonwhite employment increased 9.8 percent; in 1965, General Motors' domestic employment increase 6.4 percent, nonwhite employment 14.5 percent; in 1966, the figures were a 1.1 percent in total employment, and a 9.3 percent increase in nonwhite employment.

Judged by recent events, it is reasonable to expect that the country's employer of the largest number of Negroes will continue to increase the percentage of Negroes in its employee force.

THE NEGRO AND THE UAW

Employment policies in the automobile industry are primarily management functions, but a union as powerful as the United Automobile, Aerospace and Agricultural Implement Workers plays a significant role. Hiring is done by management. If, however, discrimination is exercised in promotion, or if opportunities are denied to Negroes, the grievance machinery is available for redress and union officials, local and national, are expected to assess the grievance and to press it if it has a basis in fact.

The UAW has always prided itself on its nondiscriminatory stance. During World War II, for example, as already noted, although considerably less powerful than today, UAW officers vigorously opposed strikes aimed at preventing the upgrading of Negroes, and strongly supported the demands of Negroes for expanded employment opportunities. The seniority rules now extant in the industry permit as wide opportunities as exist anywhere in industry for intraplant and area interplant movement. There can be no doubt that these seniority regulations have been a significant factor in the expansion of Negro production jobs. Moreover, except at Chrysler, the UAW does not have any significant bargaining rights among salaried personnel; hence it cannot be charged with responsibility in this area of employment, although, among clerical groups, nonunion Ford, not partially unionized Chrysler, is the leading employer of Negroes.

The international UAW officials, and particularly President Walter Reuther, have always also been strong supporters of such Negro aspirations as equality in jobs, housing, and in other economic, political, and social activities, both within and outside of union affairs. Negroes have been appointed to a variety of union offices in the UAW, and have won numerous local elective offices. Few unions have made equality of opportunity and union performance so significant a union policy and activity as has the UAW. Nevertheless, Professor F. Ray Marshall, certainly a friendly observer of the UAW, found considerable dissatisfaction among Negro union members about the effectiveness of the UAW stance in the late 1950's and early 1960's.[52] The roots of the problem go back to World War II, or even earlier.

In our discussion of the early period, it was noted that the attitude of Negroes toward the UAW was initially one of watchful waiting and suspicion. Then after Ford was unionized, Negroes became a force strong enough to demand redress of their special problems in UAW conventions. The strikes incident to Negro upgrading during World War II convinced Negro UAW members that they needed a Negro on the UAW international executive board to protect their interests. At this time, the UAW was split into two factions: the Reuther and the Addes or left wing group. Mr. Reuther refused to support the creation of a "Negro job"; Addes did, and Negroes provided his margin of re-election in 1943, but the provision for a Negro executive board member was defeated.[53]

---

52. Marshall, *op. cit.*, pp. 68-69, 83-84, and 178-179.
53. See Bailer, "The Automobile Unions and Negro Labor," *op. cit.*, pp. 572-575; Marshall, *op. cit.*, pp. 83-84; and Irving Howe and B. J. Widick, *The UAW and Walter Reuther* (New York: Random House, 1949), pp. 207-234.

The fight over group Negroes' special representation on the UAW board continued until 1962, when two at large members were elected, one Negro and one Canadian. In the meantime, Mr. Reuther eliminated his rivals and won complete control of the UAW. As a compromise, a UAW Fair Practices and Anti-Discrimination Department was established in 1946, and Mr. Reuther and other top union officials continued to give their unqualified support to full equality and treatment for Negro union members.

Negro dissatisfaction, however, remained. It apparently was based upon the failure to achieve a number of objectives, and the feeling among some Negroes that the union Fair Practices and Anti-Discrimination Department was, as some put it, "ceremonial and symbolic."[54]

Some of the Negro UAW members' dissatisfaction undoubtedly came from the fact that their leverage as a minority was reduced after the war when Mr. Reuther swept his opposition out of office. For a time prior to that, Negroes controlled a balance of power bloc at UAW conventions, and in some key locals. After the Reuther victory, this no longer was true. Moreover, in local elections at Ford Local 600 as well as elsewhere, race bloc voting seems to have increased racial tension and not been too successful from the Negro point of view.[55] Of course, as the proportion of Negroes tends to increase in many plants, such voting can insure the election of Negroes to local offices. Bloc voting, however, seems certain to worsen race relations in the union.

Particular dissatisfaction for Negroes in the period prior to 1963 was the failure of the UAW to insist in integrating southern locals, especially the General Motors local in Atlanta. The tensions there have already been noted, and contrasted with the International Harvester situation at Memphis.

The UAW, strangely enough, has acted more vigorously in opposing southern local segregation and discrimination among nonautomobile locals than among automobile locals. Besides trusteeing the Harvester local at Memphis, it revoked the charter of a Dallas local in 1952 composed of Braniff Airline mechanical employees.[56] The latter action proved largely futile. The Braniff employees obtained a charter from the International Association of Machinists, which

---

54. Marshall, *op. cit.*, p. 69.
55. *Ibid.*
56. *Ibid.*, p. 178; and personal investigation, October 1967.

then won bargaining rights, and the Negro employees involved ended up with a union definitely less interested in altering the *status quo.*

Obviously, the UAW went along with discrimination in Atlanta. Yet unless the company takes the lead, as Harvester did at Memphis, or as General Motors did later in Atlanta, the union cannot do the job. Its role is largely supportive in such a situation, but its support can, of course, also be crucial or even necessary.

Another Negro grievance is based upon the belief that the UAW skilled trades group has limited Negro employment opportunities. This charge is more difficult to assess, although the widespread claim that discrimination existed and the absence of Negroes from any large-scale participation in apprentice training gives some credence to their charges.

The skilled trades group has always been a problem to the UAW because of its strategic significance in bargaining and strike situations and its uneasy alliance with production workers. Essentially craft minded, and considering themselves socially above the production workers, the skilled trades group has often threatened to secede from the UAW and join various craft unions. The ideology of the group, like that of the building trades craftsmen, essentially rejects equality of opportunity in favor of an elite corps maintained in part by excluding "undesirables" and limiting entrance to trades.

The skilled trades group has power in the UAW beyond numbers. They have now even been acceded the right to reject contracts and make that rejection binding on the majority—a UAW constitutional provision of questionable legality.[57] UAW leadership has been forced to tread lightly in forcing its views on the skilled craftsmen who historically at least have not as a group been committed to equality of opportunity.

The UAW's Fair Practices and Anti-Discrimination Department, which was established in 1946, is supported by a special fund of 1 percent per member per month. According to Professor Marshall, Negro UAW members have had mixed feelings concerning the Department.[58] Proponents felt that the Department symbolized the UAW's interest and good intentions and attracted race relations ex-

---

57. Should a contract be rejected because the skilled trades reject it even though a majority in the bargaining unit accepts it, it is possible that the UAW can be charged with bargaining in bad faith—a violation of Section 8(b)(3) of the Taft-Hartley Act.

58. Marshall, *op. cit.,* pp. 83-84.

perts to work on problems. Opponents felt that the Department was "window dressing" that excused the union from acting.

In fact, the Fair Practices Department seems to have dramatized the UAW's commitment, and to have provided the UAW leadership with facts and programs. Its role has been more educational than action-oriented.

Negroes aggrieved over alleged discriminatory employment practices—as differentiated from union practices—need not utilize the Fair Practices Department, but can rather (and generally do) process their complaint through the regular grievance machinery. All automobile-company-UAW contracts contain an antidiscrimination clause similar to the one found in the General Motors contract:

> It is the policy of General Motors and the UAW-AFL-CIO that the provisions of this Agreement be applied to all employees covered by this Agreement without regard to race, color, creed or national origin. Any claims of violation of this policy may be taken up as a grievance, provided that any such claim must be supported by written evidence by the time it is presented by the Shop Committee at a meeting with Management.

Of course, if a company official is discriminatory, and the local union committeemen and officials condone or support such discrimination, even such a clause as this may not be helpful. Its very existence, however, provides the opportunity to redress wrongs.

Although the function of the Fair Practices Department is, in fact, primarily educational, this is, indeed, a prime need. As Howe and Widick stated: "The blunt truth is that the bulk of the prejudice in the UAW is to be found in the ranks. . . . "[59] The same men who work next to Negroes in a plant may refuse to socialize with them on the outside or live in areas which have Negroes. The fact that Negroes must commute long distances to work in suburban plants because of such housing discrimination embitters relations within the plants; it also keeps down Negro participation in union affairs for local union halls are found near the place of work. Commuting long distances can insure lack of attendance at meetings. Negro spokesmen have expressed concern at the "apathy" of a large percentage of Negro union members.[60] Undoubtedly, disinterest is furthered by

59. Howe and Widick, *op. cit.*, p. 228.
60. See, e.g., the comments of A. Philip Randolph, quoted by Marshall, *op. cit.*, p. 72.

social rebuffs and by obstacles such as lack of available housing nearby to plants and to union meeting halls.

It is easy to criticize the UAW, as it is the companies, for failing to eliminate discrimination. Yet given the political realities in which the national union officials must operate, and considering the accomplishments to date, one must conclude that they have led, not followed the membership, toward equal employment opportunity. It is also not surprising that local officials, coming themselves from the rank and file, and subject to re-election by that rank and file, have often stood with their constituents against progress. By and large, however, despite shortcomings, the UAW has remained throughout its existence a constructive force in the drive to reduce prejudice and to further equal employment opportunity in the industry.

CHAPTER VII

Some Personnel Problems of the New Era

It is obvious that Negroes are now a significant and permanent part of the automobile industry work force, and that the number and percentage of Negroes have not only increased substantially in recent years, but are very likely to continue to do so. This raises the question of what problems have occurred as a result of the changing racial employment composition in the industry. At least three deserve special analysis: the impact on white employees, the effect on efficiency and turnover, and the discipline problem.

Detroit in 1967, as in 1943, was the scene of a destructive and senseless riot. The impact of this riot on Negro employment opportunities and company personnel policies is also discussed in this chapter.

IMPACT ON WHITE EMPLOYEES

Employers have found that when a department or plant becomes heavily Negro, whites no longer seek employment there. There is an analogy to housing. As more Negroes move in, fewer whites seek to live in a neighborhood. The high wages of the automobile industry hold the white workers already in plants, but as the percentage of Negroes approaches one half, new white worker applications decline and those who apply tend not to stay long. Progressively, the operation becomes more heavily Negro. This is a phenomenon which this author has observed in a number of plants in various industries.

The difficulties which Negroes often encounter in trying to break into formerly all white jobs are well-known. They have been brutalized, jostled, socially ostracized, and made the butt of jokes, horseplay, and vicious behavior. Such things have occurred in the automobile industry and could even occur today in subtle forms. Now in some plants the shoe is on the other foot. Jostling of white workers by the Negro majority has induced white workers to leave some plants, and fear of such behavior keeps other whites from applying.

But jostling is probably not the basic reason why some plants, particularly in the Detroit area, will continue to become more heavily Negro. When plants move toward a Negro majority, this fact becomes known and whites do not apply, or do not stay if they are hired. In a tight labor market this is accentuated. With plants located both in suburbs and city, as is the case of the Detroit area, the suburban dwelling whites can seek employment near their homes, the city dwelling Negroes near theirs. Interplant labor pool arrangements offset these movements somewhat; but the city plants, or particular departments which reach a high percentage of Negroes, continue to have a declining white ratio.

Managements are, of course, concerned about this trend. They have been working assiduously for equal employment opportunity, especially since 1960, but the tendency of some plants and departments to become overwhelmingly Negro, is a trend toward segregation. Moreover, it also narrows the labor market from which employees may be drawn as whites are eliminated as contenders for some jobs, the labor force potential is downgraded because of the disadvantaged educational backgrounds of Negroes, and the large numbers of Negro applicants without industrial experience.

This situation should not be overstressed in so far as the automobile industry is concerned. It is mainly a Detroit area phenomenon now. Negroes are overall still a minority of the production workers in the industry as a whole. Moreover, the plants in Detroit are among the oldest in the industry. As new ones are built, they will be most probably located in outlying areas. Negroes will continue to work in such plants, but a substantial white local force will be available also. Nevertheless, the reluctance of white workers to work in plants which become known as "Negro plants," is likely to continue.

EFFICIENCY AND TURNOVER

The automobile industry added more than 250,000 persons to its rolls between 1960 and 1966, but to do so it employed probably about 1.5 million persons. A sizable proportion of these more than one million hires are Negroes. Data concerning the relative efficiency of Negroes and whites are not available, but such problems as turnover, sickness and accident claims, seem to point in one direction—a higher turnover of Negroes, much greater incidence of claims, and a variety of problems related thereto.

Management personnel questioned were unanimous that the turnover of Negroes was much higher than whites, but they also stressed that this was particularly the case with the newly hired. The Negro employees who had been with the companies for a number of years were fairly stable. If a person remained more than one year he usually settled down. For example, Ford officials report that turnover, absenteeism, and other problems at the River Rouge foundry, where a great majority of the employees are colored, are well within reasonable bounds. Here the labor force is older, and young persons added to the labor force have ample opportunity to observe good working habits and attitudes of older persons of their own race. In addition a very competent plant personnel manager, himself a Negro, is given considerable credit for the stability of the operation. Yet despite such exceptions, turnover and absenteeism have remained excessive. To obtain one permanent employee since 1965, companies have been compelled to hire four or six.

In suburban plants, some of the same problems occurred with young white workers. "They looked at this pretty new plant, and applied for work. Then they found out that they were expected to work hard; they often lasted only a few weeks." Thus did a plant manager comment on some of his new white employees in March 1967. Said the personnel man in the same plant: "In Detroit, the heavy turnover, the Monday absentees, and the sickness and accident claims were dominated by Negroes; in this suburban paradise, the young white boys give them competition for these dubious traits."[61]

It is difficult to distinguish the youth trait from the Negro one, for young Negroes are heavily represented in the new labor force in the Detroit area. Most management personnel contacted felt, however, that jobs with high earnings were so new to the young Negroes, who had rarely seen such earning capacity in their families or in their neighborhoods that they easily enjoyed it and spent it loosely, often becoming either incapacitated for Monday work, or felt that they were so rich that they stayed off the job for days after payday. Said one labor relations official: "If we disciplined for days off and tardiness like we should, we would not have a labor force."

---

61. Interviews were conducted during November and December 1966, during the first half of 1967, and in January 1968.

Moreover, since work has not been available to young Negroes heretofore, especially with the pace, discipline, and need for physical stamina of an automotive factory, they often easily decide that the work is too rigorous and quit. The resultant turnover is enormous. To add one hundred, meant hiring four hundred, and in some plants, six hundred. The high turnover continues.

Of particular interest, was the belief among management personnel that newly arrived Negro migrants from the South were turning out to be superior employees to those who grew up in the cities. It is customary to blame inferior southern conditions for much of the employment and social problems which Negroes encounter in industry and in city living. Certainly this is often a correct analysis. But the automobile companies have found that many southern Negroes, for all their disabilities, are able and willing to work for a day's pay, whereas the city-bred Negroes are less likely to have this trait.

The same distinction was noted by a suburban Detroit plant manager between white youths raised in suburbia and those raised on farms or in small towns. The latter were inevitably the best workers and the ones with the least turnover. Modern city life can discourage work aptitude and good work habits. And since Negroes tend more and more to be concentrated in the worst parts of the cities, the effect on their potential as employees is serious.

DISCIPLINE PROBLEMS

The introduction of large numbers of Negroes into huge automobile plants has brought with it the mores of the slums—violence, gambling, lawlessness—which have proved difficult to control. Although the companies are understandably reticent on this subject, some plant managers and personnel officials indicated the concern felt. In one plant, there have been knifings, three shootings, and numerous thefts. Gambling is a constant problem. Parking lot thefts are so bad in some plants that the UAW has become interested in a group automobile insurance program to offset rising insurance rates. With so many new employees, and so many of these never before holding good jobs and being associated with relative prosperity and material well-being, the behavior and actions represent from whence they have come not where they are. The rising crime rate in our cities, particularly in the slum areas, is thus being carried into the plants.

Under these circumstances, it is no wonder that plant discipline and efficiency have suffered, and that quality has been hurt. Lack of experience, and lack of association directly or through the work of parents, with machinery and with industrial behavior, a poor education in northern city slums or in southern segregated schools, all greatly complicate the Negro automobile workers' learning experiences. Long hours—six and seven days a week, nine and ten hours a day— inflate workers' earnings, but add to the fatigue, absenteeism, and general disinterest, which hurt efficiency and quality. Moreover, the expansion of employment has resulted in the upgrading to supervision of thousands who are inexperienced at managing. Supervisors, on occasion, faced with violent reactions of employees fresh from the slums, have backed down in fear and discipline has suffered.

In time, the situation in some of these automobile plants will undoubtedly achieve a reasonable equilibrium. High earnings seem certain to stabilize the lives and habits of young Negro employees who grew up on relief or on southern farms, and without hopes of achieving what is already theirs. Nevertheless, the companies now realize that they must face up to new discipline problems before they become even more serious.

One must conclude, therefore, that the current employment of large numbers of Negroes has hurt efficiency and quality. In perspective, however, one may also hope that like all other newcomers to the industry, including the Negroes who joined the automobile labor force during World War II period, the new-Negro automobile workers will settle down to productive efficiency and stable employment. If that occurs, the Negroes in America will have achieved even greater progress and a stabilizing influence.

THE IMPACT OF THE 1967 RIOT

The horrible riot which shook Detroit and the country in July 1967, had a profound effect on the automobile manufacturers. Looting occurred near Chrysler headquarters and plants, and within easy range of the General Motors headquarters. Plants were shut down or nearly so because personnel feared to traverse riot-torn areas. As in 1943, no disturbances occurred in any plants, nor in or around the suburban headquarters of Ford at Dearborn, but Ford also lost production because of absenteeism.

Although looting and rioting remained outside of factory walls, some automobile workers, again as in 1943, were involved and arrested as looters. That such rioting and looting occurred in the city where Negroes have as good, if not better, industrial employment opportunities than anywhere in the world seemed surprising. Yet the riot of 1943 also occurred in a period of relatively full employment and expanding job opportunities.

High employment and expanding job opportunities affect race relations in contradictory ways. The tensions over job competition recede when work is plentiful for all. But new job opportunities expand the horizons and aspirations of Negro workers and at least temporarily create new crises by altering the *status quo*. Racial antagonism can then easily surface. Detroit has had two horrible race riots in times of relatively full employment—none in a recession.

Immediately after the rioting ended, all the automobile companies began not only to cooperate with government and UAW officials to try to prevent a recurrence of lawlessness, but also to re-examine hiring policies. Despite the fact that their hiring standards have encouraged the employment of unskilled in very large numbers, all companies have since made their standards even more flexible. Chrysler, for example, dropped previous barriers against persons with nondangerous or minor police records in order to open up jobs to Negroes who had had scrapes with the law. Chrysler "adopted" a high school in center city Detroit, in order to aid in instruction and to encourage students to stay in school and to look to the automobile industry for employment. Chrysler also stepped up its Detroit hiring and adopted and publicized its new policy to expand the number of Negro dealers.

In three months after the riot, General Motors hired 12,200 in the Detroit and Pontiac areas, 5,300 of whom were Negroes. For the first time General Motors went into Negro areas and hired on the spot, and also took referrals from government manpower and antipoverty agencies. According to General Motors Chairman, James M. Roche, continued adherence to a nondiscriminatory employment policy was not enough. More had to be done than "to wait for the qualified applicant to present himself at our employment office."

In addition, General Motors also instructed its employment personnel to utilize a "rule of reason" in taking men with police records.

Special programs were initiated at Chevrolet Gear and Axle in Detroit, and at Pontiac and Fisher Body plants in Pontiac "to locate those individuals previously considered unhirable and to hire them." In Pontiac, of the first 250 hired, 182 were able to complete their probationary period, "90 percent of whom are described by supervision as 'competent' while the others need additional training."[62]

Ford also reacted energetically. It sent its employment interviewers into inner city areas and employed persons on the spot. Those that needed it were given a week's worth of bus tickets free of charge and lunch tickets for one hot meal, the cost of which is deducted from the second and third pay check. Some 3,000 Negroes were thus hired by the end of January 1968, nearly all of them at the River Rouge works. Of the 3,000, 1,600 were on the job; 600 were awaiting job assignment; 425 were rejected after physical examinations or were found to have major or habitual criminal records; and 375 who were hired either never showed up or "are taking their time about showing up for work."[63]

In addition to those hired by interviewers within the inner city, Ford hired some 2,800 persons—walk-in hires—at Detroit area employment offices during the same period. Of these 1,460 are considered to have been from among the hard core unemployed, undoubtedly motivated by the publicity over the Ford program.[64]

The success of these programs will depend on many things, not the least of which is continued high sales and employment which will avoid layoffs, and the ability of the companies to overcome the turnover and discipline problems incident to the introduction of large numbers of unskilled and inexperienced personnel. To emphasize the company's commitment, Mr. Henry Ford II wrote all supervisors and executives on January 17, 1968, asking for their "full and active support" for equal opportunity in "one of Ford Motor Company's oldest, firmest and most basic policies." In this letter, Mr. Ford stated the inner-city hiring program's aim "is not only to offer employment opportunities, but actively to invite the interest of people who would not normally come to us—not to screen *out* doubtful applicants but to screen *in* if possible—and not merely to hire, but to help them make the grade after they are hired."

---

62. See *New York Times*, November 10, 1967; *Daily Labor Report*, No. 220, November 15, 1967, pp. A-7-8.

63. On the Ford program, see Gertrude Samuels, "Help Wanted: The Hard-Core Unemployed," *New York Times Magazine*, January 28, 1968, pp. 26-27, 42-50.

64. *Ibid.*

The automobile industry's program to work hard core unemployed into jobs is possible because of the large number of unskilled entry positions which its processes can utilize. Its experience will be valuable in determining America's capacity to rehabilitate through employment. Those who are hired and remain on the job for a reasonable time will be immensely more capable of shifting for themselves if automobile sales decline and layoffs occur, but the longer that they remain on the job, the more likely will they become productive citizens.

The policies announced by the automobile companies also involve a complete reversal of traditional industrial hiring practices. Employment policies have stressed the hiring of the fittest and best personnel obtainable in the labor market; now the companies are literally searching for the most marginal that possibly can be utilized. That Mr. Ford wrote his executives and supervisors stressing the change and asking their assistance is indeed understandable. Such a policy change will require complete management support if it is to succeed. And if it does succeed, it will be a milestone of company personnel policy to achieve racial integration.

CHAPTER VIII.

Determinants of Industry Policy

In the course of this study, a number of factors have been discussed which have contributed to the racial employment policies of the automobile industry. These and others should be noted again in these concluding remarks.

THE NEED FOR EMPLOYEES

Negroes have made their greatest gains in three periods of tight labor markets—World War I, World War II, and 1962-1966. The availability of Negro labor to a growing automobile industry at critical moments in the history of both the Negro worker and the industry has provided an extraordinary mutual advantage. There can be no doubt that the industry's need and their availability are the most significant facts in Negroes becoming such an important part of the industry's labor force.

THE CHARACTER OF THE WORK

In the first part of this study (Table 2) it was noted that semi-skilled operatives comprise more than one-half of the labor force, and that with laborers and service workers, an even greater majority. In few industries can inexperienced workers be utilized to such an advantage and at such attractive wages. A grade school education is usually sufficient, and sometimes necessary, for work on the assembly line. The industry affords an excellent opportunity for those without industrial experience. The nature of the work has permitted the assimilation into the work force of thousands of unskilled Negroes. In industries in which a much higher proportion of skilled employees or better educated workers are needed, for example, aerospace, this is not possible.

INDUSTRIAL LOCATION

Automobile plants tend to be concentrated in or nearby, centers of population. This is where the market is, and happily for Negroes where the centers of Negro population are. The tendency today is for large assembly plants with multiple shifts in order to reduce the plant fixed costs per unit. Moreover, the development of the fifteen automobile carrying rail car has permitted companies to increase their concentrations around Detroit and in Michigan rather than to disperse plants further. This has aided Negro employment.

Some of the oldest plants are in Detroit and some may be moved out in the future. Industry policy is to transfer workers with their plants. Such movements could, however, reduce the growth in the percentage of Negroes, but it is not likely to occur rapidly nor to have immediate significance. Plant locations are likely to continue to favor increased Negro employment, as they have in the past several years, by being reasonably near the centers of Negro population in the North and Midwest.

MANAGERIAL POLICY

One wonders how much the policies of Henry Ford account for the great advances made by Negroes in the industry. When others said Negroes could not handle skilled jobs, or whites and Negroes would not work together, he demonstrated that they were wrong. When World War II came, his example had proved what was possible. The Negro automobile worker owes much to this great pioneer.

Managerial policy between 1940 and 1960 demonstrates more of a tendency to associate itself with community mores than to stride out ahead. When World War II demanded, both for labor utilization and public policy, that all citizens be given an opportunity to work, the automobile companies easily fell into step. In the postwar years, they also stayed well within the practices of the times. Negroes held on to their gains in the industry, except where layoff or plant closings hurt all workers. In states having fair employment practice legislation, such as New York or New Jersey, the automobile companies set good examples of equal opportunity for production workers and opened up some jobs for Negro white collar personnel. These laws also emphasized the need for firm company policies rather than leaving the issue to local managerial discretion, and the companies in time adopted strong policies. In general, however, the automobile companies did little pioneering in opening up salaried jobs or in integrating southern plants prior to 1960.

The new post-1967 riot programs of the automobile companies contain some of the innovative flavor of the first Henry Ford. Here the experiment of utilizing the hard core unemployed and the very marginal worker is being attempted. Given the industry's ability to utilize unskilled personnel, this experiment could be a very important contribution toward developing ways of alleviating the problem of unemployment in our central city slums.

Automobile companies feel strongly that they must examine all policies in terms of what they perceive as marketing realities. The race issue can put a company in the center of a controversy and cost it sales. Boycotts of one company by Negroes or segregationists can do just that. The Ford Motor Company is apparently most vulnerable to such action because of the close association of the Ford family with the company. According to one business journal: "Every time Henry Ford II has made a pronouncement in behalf of Negro rights, Ford Motor Co. sales have tumbled in the South."[65] It is doubtful if the impact has been either severe or permanent thus far. None of the companies show any desire to let up on their affirmative action programs however hesitant they once might have been. After Plans for Progress was inaugurated, all three companies joined. It would be difficult today to assail one company over another on this issue. Their efforts differ, and results vary some; but the commitment to equal opportunity and the need to utilize Negro labor are similar for all three.

The alignment of marketing policies and equal employment opportunity does not imply any lack of sincerity on the part of the companies. The author has talked with numerous officials in the industry who are dedicated to improvement of the Negro's status. Rather it means that the industry has a tendency, with such exceptions as Henry Ford's innovations, to stay within the country's mood in a given period. In general, the results appear to have been quite salutary for Negro employment; but during the late 1940's and 1950's, the company's racial policies were quite cautious.

A feature of management policy in the automobile industry today is the strong central staff direction of equal employment opportunity

---

65. "Business and the Urban Community," an insert into *Business Week*, February 2, 1968, p. c4.

policy. Just as the plant manager's labor relations actions are circumscribed by company policies and monitored and carefully tutored by the central staff, so equal employment opportunity has become a key central personnel staff activity. The plant managers and their staffs and the line organizations are given direct authority for seeing that equal opportunity policies are effectuated and are held responsible for the results. They are assisted, counseled, and policed by the central staff. In each company, the "word from above" is that equal employment opportunity is important, that the job must be done, and that affirmative and innovative actions are to be encouraged. There is no reason to believe that these policies will not be continued. Sound performance in civil rights matters, like sound performance in labor relations, are now part of the line managers' jobs. Experts on the staff responsible for minority employment appear to be as permanent a fixture as the labor relations group grew to be twenty-five years ago. In the automobile industry, the companies obviously expect to be able to be concerned constructively with minority group employment in the years ahead.

GOVERNMENT POLICY

Government policy has been an important factor in strengthening Negro labor utilization in the industry. Governmental insistence on progress during World War II both prodded the companies and gave them backing for action. State fair employment practice laws, and the threat of more, helped to keep policies reasonably liberal between 1945 and 1960. The contract compliance work, Plans for Progress, and Civil Rights laws of the 1960's have insured further action since then. Government encouragement and cooperation with industry after the July 1967 riot further encouraged and aided the programs for employment of the inner city and marginal Negroes.

We have already noted the importance of government policy in eliminating distinction among companies. Ending segregation in southern plants when the school integration crisis remained heated, further offended local white citizens, employees, and often local union officials, with local management personnel sometimes joining the footdragging. It was important that this be done by all companies at once. Having Negro performers star on their television shows, or in the case of Ford, publicity about grants of the Ford Foundation (totally unrelated to the company in management but not in people's minds) to a Negro group, or statements by Henry Ford II, evoked threats of boycotts. With all major companies following government policies, such threats are much less effective, even granting Mr. Ford's visibility.

Regular government inspections also keep the issue in the fore-front. Some method of coordinating procurement agency, Equal Employment Opportunity Commission, and state agency inspections would decrease much lost time without diminishing the reminder that equal opportunity is the law. Yet plant inspections bring home to local managers the importance of the issue, for managers do not gain merit by inducing adverse rulings or publicity.

UNION POLICY

The industry is fortunate, first, in that unionization has occurred on an industrial basis and second, that its equal opportunity stance has strong support from the top officials of the UAW. Because unionization has occurred on an industrial basis, and because a majority of jobs in the plants are within a narrow spectrum of skill, seniority districts tend to become wide and in addition provide for transfer not only among departments, but among plants as well. If unionism were organized on a craft basis, or if progressions among jobs were established on long narrow bases, this would not be possible. The lack of union fragmentation, and the fluidity within the plants and among the plants provided in the union agreements have been major factors in expanding employment opportunities for Negroes.

In policy matters, Mr. Reuther and other top union officials have worked sincerely and assiduously for equal opportunity, cooperating with management officials where such cooperation was needed. There can be little doubt of their commitment.

Of course, it must be emphasized that the UAW is a labor union, not a civil rights organization. Demands, for example, that Negroes be given "superseniority" to compensate for past injustices are unthinkable for the union leadership and unsupportable by the membership which is predominantly white. Likewise attempts of Dr. Martin Luther King to win union support for a boycott against General Motors because, in his opinion, General Motors is not doing enough for civil rights, evoked instead praise for General Motors' nondiscrimination efforts from the UAW.[66] The UAW has been of definite aid in the progress of Negro automobile workers, but its prime interests remain those of a union and must be such if it is to survive, just as the prime aim of each company must be that of a profit-making corporation if it is to perform the functions of producing automobiles and providing employment.

---

66. Leonard Woodcock, UAW Vice-President, and chief negotiator in General Motors matters, was quoted in answer to Dr. King, that General Motors "had made an honest effort to practice nondiscrimination and offer opportunities to Negroes." *New York Times,* July 16, 1967.

CHAPTER IX.

Concluding Remarks

Negro workers play a major role in the automobile industry. Moreover, the situation remains very favorable not only for a continuation but an improvement in this situation. Of course there are problems involved and obstacles to overcome. A downturn in the industry's sales could reduce the proportion of Negroes at least temporarily, and so could a movement away from cities. Neither appears likely, however, to offset the great increases of the last several years. Cutbacks in early 1967, for example, resulted in layoffs of several thousand, about 80 percent of whom were low seniority Negroes. Attrition and turnover, however, soon returned many of these to jobs. As Negroes continue to hold down jobs in large numbers, their confidence and abilities will grow, and they will progress despite any temporary setback. It would appear, therefore, that the years ahead will see increased participation of Negroes in skilled, office, and salaried positions while they increase their share of production jobs.

Index

INDUSTRIAL RESEARCH UNIT
DEPARTMENT OF INDUSTRY
WHARTON SCHOOL OF FINANCE AND COMMERCE
UNIVERSITY OF PENNSYLVANIA

The Industrial Research Unit is the business and labor research arm of the Department of Industry, Wharton School of Finance and Commerce. Founded in 1921 after World War I as a separate Wharton School Department, the Industrial Research Unit has a long record of publication and research in the labor market, productivity, union relations, and business report fields. Major Industrial Research Unit Studies are published as research projects are completed. Advance research reports are issued as appropriate in a general or special series.

Recent Major Industrial Research Unit Studies

Gladys L. Palmer, et al., *The Reluctant Job Changer.* 1962.   No. 40 $7.50

George M. Parks, *The Economics of Carpeting and Resilient Flooring: An Evaluation and Comparison.* 1966.   No. 41 $1.50 (Paper)

Michael H. Moskow, *Teachers and Unions: The Applicability of Collective Bargaining to Public Education.* 1966.   No. 42 $8.50 (Cloth)   5.95 (Paper)

F. Marion Fletcher, *Market Restraints in the Retail Drug Industry.* 1967.   No. 43 $10.00

Herbert R. Northrup and Gordon R. Storholm, *Restrictive Labor Practices in the Supermarket Industry.* 1967.   No. 44 $7.50

Published by
University of Pennsylvania Press
Philadelphia, Pennsylvania 19104

Research Report Series

Racial Policies in American Industry Series

1. *The Negro in the Automobile Industry,* by Herbert R. Northrup. 1968. $2.50
Forthcoming Racial Policies reports will include aerospace, iron and steel, petroleum, rubber tires, pulp and paper, banking, retail stores, and insurance.

Labor Relations and Public Policy Series

1. *Compulsory Arbitration and the NLRB,* by Paul A. Abodeely. 1968. $2.50
Forthcoming studies will deal with various aspects of government labor policy including recognition by card check, bargaining unit determination, and government intervention in labor disputes.

Miscellaneous Series

14. *Economics of Carpeting and Resilient Flooring: A Survey of Published Material and a Questionnaire Summary,* by David C. Stewart. 1966. $1.00

15. *Job Mobility and Occupational Change: Philadelphia Male Workers, 1940-1960,* by Carol P. Brainerd. 1966. $2.00

Order from
University of Pennsylvania Press
Philadelphia, Pennsylvania 19104